To my Artie, with love and gratitude, from your Olive.

Arrival of the Light Beings

How to Prepare for the Shift and Contact with Extraterrestrials

LINDA HALEY

BALBOA.PRESS
A DIVISION OF HAY HOUSE

Balboa Press books may be ordered through booksellers or by contacting:

Balboa Press
A Division of Hay House
1663 Liberty Drive
Bloomington, IN 47403
www.balboapress.com
844-682-1282

Because of the dynamic nature of the Internet, any web addresses or links contained in this book may have changed since publication and may no longer be valid. The views expressed in this work are solely those of the author and do not necessarily reflect the views of the publisher, and the publisher hereby disclaims any responsibility for them.

The author of this book does not dispense medical advice or prescribe the use of any technique as a form of treatment for physical, emotional, or medical problems without the advice of a physician, either directly or indirectly. The intent of the author is only to offer information of a general nature to help you in your quest for emotional and spiritual well-being. In the event you use any of the information in this book for yourself, which is your constitutional right, the author and the publisher assume no responsibility for your actions.

Cover design by C Bean and C Zellers.
For more information, please go to www.lindahaley.net

Print information available on the last page.

ISBN: 978-1-9822-6791-9 (sc)
ISBN: 978-1-9822-6793-3 (hc)
ISBN: 978-1-9822-6792-6 (e)

Library of Congress Control Number: 2021908194

Balboa Press rev. date: 05/24/2021

Contents

....

Preface ix

Prologue xi

Part 1
Awareness

Chapter 1   It's Time 1

Chapter 2   Visitors in the Dark 3

Chapter 3   Taken... 5

Chapter 4   Childhood Terrors 11

Chapter 5   Chloe...15

Chapter 6   Starseed Connection 19

Chapter 7   The Importance of Protection..................... 23

Chapter 8   Artie 29

Chapter 9   Spirituality versus Religion 33

Chapter 10   Spirit Releasements 39

Chapter 11   Soon Arrive.. 47

Chapter 12   Avratar.. 51

Chapter 13   Is All This Real? 59

Chapter 14   Gaia Is Hurting 65

Chapter 15   Other Lives.. 69

Part 2
Awakening

Chapter 16 Quieting the Mind 75
Chapter 17 Different Beings.. 81
Chapter 18 Opening the Third Eye.. 89
Chapter 19 Chakras 97

Part 3
Arrival

Chapter 20 Critically Important...117
Chapter 21 Reptilian in the MRI 131
Chapter 22 Why Are You Coming?..141
Chapter 23 Your Help Is Needed..155
Chapter 24 No Reason to Fear 161
Chapter 25 Preparing the Heart 165
Chapter 26 Arrival 181

Preface

....

I didn't plan on writing a book, but then again, I also didn't plan on being contacted by extraterrestrials. Writing a book was Avratar's idea.

"Why me?" I asked.

He explained patiently that I understood the fear of the unknown, especially the fear of anything extraterrestrial. They needed my help in making others understand why they were coming and in detailing the many reasons Earth needed them at this time.

I suppose I must have been the ideal challenge to be transformed into a believer. I was a hard-core skeptic. I confused religion with spirituality. Life in a haunted house led me to consciously avoid anything that was even remotely scary or unknown. I certainly wanted nothing to do with ETs.

Just about everything in this book really happened to me, even the scary parts, but I thought it would be far more engaging if it were Olive's story. Watching Olive's growing awareness was an opportunity for me to recall the details of my own evolution.

Far too many books and movies paint dire consequences as the result of any interaction with off-world beings. In almost every case, the interaction doesn't end well for the humans. I believe in a more positive outcome, and I believe the messages being received worldwide are accurate: Earth is in trouble, and aid is arriving like the galactic Red Cross. The physical and energetic changes Earth is experiencing are reflected in the lives of her occupants. Both Earth and her humans are beginning to be impacted by a massive shift in consciousness, often called the ascension.

This book is not for those who already fully understand and embrace what is happening on Earth right now. It is also not for those who don't care.

It is for those whose minds and souls are receptive to welcoming the concept that humans are not alone in the universe and that we will soon be meeting our cosmic cousins in peace and gratitude.

Prologue

....

"What do I call you?" she asked. "Visitors? Multidimensional beings?"

She had heard that they didn't like to be called *aliens*—she supposed that made sense, as they probably saw humans as alien—and *extraterrestrial* seemed sterile and cumbersome, as though a scientist had put a noncommittal label on something he didn't fully understand.

"We are not visitors," he responded quietly. "We are part of the fabric of your culture."

She paused and then realized that was probably true. They had been there as long as the planet.

"You may call us friends."

There was another pause as she thought about his words. She didn't quite understand their relationship but thought they definitely had become friends—in an extraterrestrial kind of way.

It took quite a while, maybe several years, for her to believe she was actually in contact with someone from another dimension. Or maybe it was another planet. She wasn't sure. It took even longer for her to have the courage to tell others. She hoped it would be different this time, because it hadn't gone well before. There had been whispering and concern. Had she gotten into drugs? Maybe she was looking for attention, or possibly these were the first signs of mental illness. In the beginning, she'd wondered if they were right. Was she perhaps going crazy? Now she was asked to publicly talk about everything.

"Tell your story," he said. "They must understand that we are here to help."

She wondered if she had a choice. After all, humans were supposed to have free will, weren't they? Didn't he realize how much she was dreading this? He probably did, since he already had asked her twice, "What is your perceived blockage?" She wasn't sure if she was being gently reassured or seriously reprimanded. She couldn't figure out how he even knew she hadn't started the book. But then she realized he seemed to know pretty much everything, including everything that had happened to her throughout her entire life. *He probably also knows what is coming for all of us*, she thought.

She was afraid it would be worse for her this time, especially since even more people would know, and she had much more to tell. Why did she feel such urgency? Did she realize it on her own or hear it in the messages to her? She wasn't sure.

She would be ridiculed by people who didn't even know her. She could handle that, she supposed. *But what happens if they hate me or worse? What happens if they're angered by what I have to say?* There were things that some people didn't want to hear, and there were people who didn't want anyone to know. But she also knew there would be many people who wanted—and needed—to hear the message.

This was important to him—to all of them. Actually, his exact words had been *critically important*. It must have been pretty serious for them to come all this way just to help. She wasn't sure why it was so important or what role she played in this massive cosmic chess game, but she had always listened to her vibes. Even the tiny part she knew about was overwhelming. She wasn't sure if she wanted to know more.

He also had said more than once, "Time is limited." She suspected that was the reason for the sense of urgency. She wasn't sure how to communicate that urgency, when she wasn't really sure what was coming.

She also wasn't sure how to even begin or which incidents she should share. What about all the scary times? Should she even mention the terrifying experiences in the dead of night, the unexplained marks on her body, or the things she'd seen right in front of her that weren't supposed to exist? She had spent a lifetime trying to forget. Now having to remember just to tell others made her sick.

"Tell everything. Those experiences are part of your story."

For some reason, her story was part of his story and the greater story. Maybe that had been part of the plan all along. She had no doubt that her experiences had really happened, so all she had to do was tell others how she had gotten from there to here.

This is her story.

Part 1

Awareness

Chapter 1

It's Time

....

The dizziness didn't concern her as much as the weird sound. She knew she hadn't had much to drink the night before—maybe a couple of glasses of wine. But the sound was odd and also a little frightening, especially since the others didn't seem to hear it. It sounded like the whoosh of a heavy gale whipping past her. Except she was sitting in the middle of the living room, not on a windswept prairie.

"You okay in there?" Artie asked.

"Yeah! No! I don't know!" Olive yelled back. "I'll be in soon."

She tried to focus on the New Year's Day football chatter on TV instead of the wind. *Focus on the announcers. Focus on your breathing. Probably something you ate. Too many foods to know what it was.* Maybe this was how a stroke started.

The wind started to die down a bit. She could hear laughter coming from the kitchen, and she considered joining the group. Then she heard a quiet but decisive voice speak above the wind: "It's time."

She was pretty sure she had heard it inside her head, but then she really wasn't sure she had heard it at all. Maybe it was something on the TV. Maybe she was coming down with the flu. In any case, she wouldn't mention it. *People who hear voices ...* She didn't want to go there.

But then it happened a second time and then a third time five minutes later. The same voice with the same message. Firm and decisive but not unkind. There was no doubt anymore. She really had heard it, and for

1

some reason, it seemed to be directed at her. Something was talking to the inside of her head. It seemingly was giving her notice, letting her know that it was time, but for what? All she knew was that she didn't want to have any part of it, whatever it was. She liked her life just the way it was.

It wasn't important enough to tell Artie and the others. Besides, they wouldn't have believed her anyway.

Years later, she heard the voice again. She had occasionally thought about the incident on New Year's Day but had decided that since it never had happened again, maybe it really had been a hangover after all. *What a lightweight*, she'd thought. *A little wine, and I start hallucinating.* But this time, it happened in the middle of the day, in the middle of the office hallway.

Thank God there were others nearby this time to confirm the odd wind sound. The debate continued for the rest of the day.

"It was like a freight train."

"No, it was more like a hundred brooms sweeping at once."

"It sounded exciting, mysterious, and otherworldly."

Even a group of visitors heard it. Someone from maintenance eventually said it was a problem with the HVAC, and the excitement died down as quickly as the wind had.

But no one else had received the message deep inside their heads. In fact, they stared at her in a baffled sort of way when she asked. "Really," she said, "didn't any of you hear what he said?"

"Who? You're hearing voices?"

If she kept asking, they would look at her the same way the others had so long ago. It was safer to make a joke and move on.

But she had heard it. It was just like before: "It's time." It was the same voice. This time, she couldn't dismiss it as too much wine, tiredness, or anything else. This time, there was no doubt that it was time for something to happen.

A wave of anxiety swept over her.

Chapter 2

Visitors in the Dark

....

It had been a good day. She didn't mind leaving the office so late, especially since this job helped to pay for all the purchases for the house. She had only been in her new place for a few months, but she already felt she had created a sanctuary from the craziness of her work life. It wasn't fancy, just a small two-story home in an older, comfortable neighborhood. But it was hers, or it would be in another twenty-nine years.

She was still too awake to settle down for the night, so she kicked off her heels and flopped onto the couch with a cup of tea. She enjoyed management, especially the way she and her team worked together. She had been with the company for almost five years, and she didn't see any reason to leave at this point. She prided herself on thinking quickly and finding solutions, which, thankfully, were traits her bosses also seemed to like.

She took her tea upstairs to finish in bed, slipped between the covers, and started to mentally prepare for the morning meeting. She never worried about late-comers to her meetings since everyone knew the person who arrived last had to lead the morning meditation. Some of the impromptu meditations were funny, she thought, especially with some of the comedians on her staff.

Her attention went to a creak in the upstairs hallway, but odd sounds were pretty common in an old house. This house dated to the 1920s, and the old floorboards often creaked and moaned as temperatures dipped at night. It was one of the home's many charms, along with outdated plumbing, cracked plaster walls, and too few electrical outlets.

But the second creak didn't sound like the house settling. It sounded like when she walked from the stairs to the bedroom. One floorboard had a distinctive groan when she stepped on it. She stopped breathing and listened for more creaks. She was sure her pounding heart would drown out any noises from the hallway. Small beads of sweat broke out on her forehead.

Another creak. Then another. Now she was certain the sounds were closer. Someone was in the house. But the doors were all locked, and the house alarm was set. *Oh God.* Horror set in when she realized someone might have gotten in through an upstairs window. She had gotten in the habit of locking her bedroom door at night, even with the house alarm. At least there was that protection.

Terror was turning into full-blown panic, and she had to do something quickly. The phone was only a few inches away on the nightstand. Ever since college, she had slept with at least one light on. Too many bad things happened in total darkness.

Think fast. The window behind her was painted shut, so she couldn't even escape onto the roof. She picked up the phone but then froze when the old skeleton key in the bedroom door started to rattle around in the lock. Before she could dial, her entire body became immobilized with fear. It was as though an evil mist had filled the room and paralyzed every muscle. All she could do was stare into the shadows.

The skeleton key dropped with a metallic clink onto the bedroom floor, and the door opened. The last thing she saw was the figures coming into the room.

Chapter 3

Taken

....

The incessant ringing of her cell phone brought her back to consciousness. At first, she wasn't sure where she was. Her eyes hurt, as though she had worn her contacts too long, and she had a pounding headache. She felt drugged and thought she might throw up. She found the phone and grunted.

"Olive, are you okay?" her assistant asked, practically screaming into the phone. "Where are you? The meeting was supposed to start ten minutes ago."

Things were beginning to come into focus. "I'm really sorry," she stammered. "I must have overslept. Let's cancel the meeting. Tell everyone I'll do the meditation next time."

"So are you still coming in? What do you want me to tell your next appointments? How about your presentation at lunch?"

"I'll be in for the luncheon meeting but probably not before," she replied. "Cover for me, will you? I owe you a big one."

Ten minutes later, her head was under a hot shower, and the nausea was starting to subside. Her head still hurt, but at least she felt functional. *I can probably fake the presentation*, she thought. *What the heck happened?* She reconstructed the evening. She recalled getting home, making tea, and falling asleep. Then the nightmares had started. Three scary-looking creatures had come into her bedroom and taken her someplace. She struggled to remember the dream, wondering if it held a clue to her illness, but it gradually faded, as dreams often did. Anyway, she was feeling a little better now.

Glancing at herself in the mirror as she dried off, she saw a long scratch on her right cheek. *That's weird*, she thought. *That had to hurt, but I don't recall scratching myself. Maybe I did get sick during the night.* Then she saw what looked like a tattoo on her left upper arm: three small orange triangles with the points coming together. Each triangle was maybe a third of an inch long, so the whole circle probably wasn't even an inch in diameter. But it hadn't been there when she went to bed.

She studied the marks, at first with curiosity and then with growing disbelief. Finally, the reality hit her that it hadn't been a dream. *Oh God, no. It had to be a dream.*

She scrubbed her arm until her skin was raw. Actually, her whole body felt raw, dirty, and violated. She was tempted to take another shower, but she knew it wouldn't help. The orange triangles were a little lighter but still there. All the terror from last night resurfaced—hearing the creaks, watching the key fall from the lock, feeling total helplessness as they came closer—and she started to cry uncontrollably. Was she crying out of fear, confusion, or what? She didn't know. But the terror penetrated every part of her, and it felt even larger than it had last night, if that were possible. She locked the bathroom door, crawled into the closet, and sobbed till her stomach hurt and she could only take gulps of air.

She furiously searched her memory for clues—anything that would help her make sense of the last twelve hours. She remembered that everything had seemed to happen in slow motion. There had been three of them, with one staying in the hallway. In her mind, she had screamed and fought, but for some reason, her body hadn't resisted. She had been unable to move, but she wasn't sure why. She'd watched everything in a detached sort of way. A random glimpse of movement, as if she were being carried without actually being touched. A flash of being on some kind of surface, maybe a table, cold and metallic. A memory of pain somewhere.

Dull, leathery gray skin—that was how she remembered them. They were not very tall, perhaps four feet, and they all looked the same. But it was the eyes she remembered the most. They seemed too big for the head, glassy or maybe shiny, and completely lifeless. Like a giant bug's eyes. They had come right into her face, and those bug eyes had been just inches from hers. The terror returned, and she furiously searched the rest of her body for orange triangles or anything else they might have done to her.

She needed to calm down. Getting all hysterical wouldn't help her figure this out. This wasn't really happening. This was still a dream. She felt as if she were in a movie—a bad movie at that. Until a few moments ago, she'd had zero reason to wonder about life on other planets. She had enough trouble in making sense of this planet. Now she wasn't sure what to think. And why her? There were probably millions of people who wanted to meet a real, live alien, so why didn't they find one of them? There were whole conventions of them, weren't there?

Was this an abduction? She had heard stories of people who had mysterious sightings of bizarre creatures and then were never seen again, women whose eggs were stolen to create hybrid children, or people who found themselves in another city or across the continent when they regained consciousness. At least she was back in her own home. But this home, her home, didn't feel safe anymore.

She had to get back to normal. *Throw on a dress, no time for makeup, and get out the door fast.* She had to get away from this house. What if they came back? What would happen the next time? She couldn't take the chance. What if they thought this was their house or there was some kind of wormhole or portal or whatever one called it in the basement? Or in the upstairs hallway just outside her bedroom door? Were they zombies? Had they attacked the previous owners too? Was that why she'd gotten such a good deal on the house?

Chloe greeted her outside her office. "Are you sure you feel good enough to be here?" she asked. "I mean, you look wiped out."

Olive mumbled something about having a bad burrito last night and reassured her she was okay. She wasn't, but she had gotten pretty good about faking it.

Olive briefly considered moving, but logic won when she calculated how much more it would cost her. She could barely afford this place. She thought about getting a roommate. Maybe the creatures would take her roommate instead. But she had the miserable feeling they would find her no matter where she lived. It was crazy, but it felt as if she had been targeted or selected. It didn't feel random. She felt trapped.

It was happening all over again. Maybe the ghosts were back. What if it wasn't the house? What if it was her? She had had ten years of feeling safe, mostly because she had willed herself to forget. The attacks were different, but the effect was the same. They always found her. They'd found her when she was a teenager and when she was a little girl.

She was going to have to find a way to feel safer here. The man installing the new bedroom door and window the next day commented on the extra locks, but she didn't feel the need to share anything with him. In fact, she hadn't shared information with anyone about that night or any other night. The fear of telling anyone was almost as intense as the fear that gripped her when she was alone when it got dark out. She had seen what happened to people who were thought to be crazy. Once a person was labeled, it was almost impossible to get beyond that.

Nighttime reminded her of the terror. It was harder to sleep with all the lights on now, but not having them on wasn't an option. Total darkness brought back the panic. She thought that maybe being in the bedroom triggered the bad memories. But sleeping downstairs in the recliner also wasn't an option; there were far too many windows to feel safe. When sleep came, it was usually from exhaustion.

She kept the bedroom door locked all the time when she was in the room. This wasn't like being at her parents' home, where someone could come in and save her. She avoided unlocking the door until daylight came; she had convinced herself she was safe when the sun came up. She wasn't sure where that belief came from, but if she had to believe something to get her through the night, that was going to be it. Going to the bathroom in the middle of the night felt like an act of extreme bravery.

The worst part was that it hadn't stopped with that awful night. Every nerve was on high alert since she never knew when something would happen or how bad it would be. Locking the door was useless; they still somehow came into her bedroom. Did they come in through the walls or squeeze in through a tiny crack? Sometimes she saw things move; other times she just heard them. She always pretended she was asleep, barely breathing, in the hope she would be left alone this time. Once, something bumped into her dresser, knocking over a perfume bottle. She heard a soft thud on the side of her closet. Things moved on her bedside table. Once, she rolled over in bed, and her arm hit something solid that shouldn't have been there. That was an especially bad night.

Sometimes there were strange lights of different sizes and sounds, such as a whine or something mechanical. Deep chills were sometimes felt on her feet or an arm—maybe when one got closer. Occasionally, she was certain she was being touched. *Do they breathe like we do?* Because she was sure she once felt soft puffs of air on her face.

When her cell phone kept getting dragged off the bedside table every night for weeks, she was sure they knew she was faking being asleep. A new level of fear gripped her. Could they read her mind? Were they slowly torturing her? Was this to make her go crazy? Maybe this was all a game to them, like playing cat and mouse. If this was a game, she didn't know the rules or even whom she was playing against.

Then there was a chattering sound like a squirrel to the right of her bed. *I'm sleeping. I'm sleeping. I can't hear you.* But then a second chattering at the foot of the bed sounded as if something answered. *Oh God, there are two of them. Maybe more. I'm sleeping. I'm sleeping.*

But the worst part was that she still saw the creatures, mostly in nightmares. Sometimes she got a flash of a memory of that night—maybe something she hadn't previously recalled. There were other people there too—other humans, not just those awful creatures. Had they also been abducted? She wondered what their lives were like now. Did they also sometimes feel as if their lives had been torn apart? She could handle the occasional bad dream; waking up in a cold sweat was becoming a regular occurrence. But sometimes images didn't feel like a dream, especially when she could clearly see something mere inches from her face as she woke up. Were they staring into her face and willing her to wake up? Sometimes it was the one she had seen before, the leathery gray one. Sometimes they were different colors or shapes, short or taller. They were almost human-looking or sometimes like something out of a bad movie. It seemed every morning brought a different alien creature. Was any of this real, or was she really going crazy after all? Was it possible that all of this was just happening in her mind?

Barney was supposed to be a guard dog, and perhaps he would have been if he'd stayed awake more. In the beginning, he would stare and growl at empty space, a sentry on patrol, and then look back at her in confusion.

His reaction to unfamiliar sights and sounds was oddly reassuring to her since it validated that things really were happening. Unfortunately, after a few nights of not seeing anything to growl at, he usually spent the night snoring in a corner. Now she loved him more for his companionship than protection. She also worried that now she had to protect him as well as herself. Would they hurt him on their way to get her?

She never had considered herself to be religious but now fervently prayed every evening to be safe. *God, please keep me safe tonight. Please, please, please.* Hadn't somebody once said there were no atheists in foxholes? She understood that because she felt she was under attack. She wasn't even sure whom she was praying to, but if something unseen was hurting her, then maybe something unseen could help. *Please, God. Please, please, please, God. Make them go away. Give me one night, just one night, when I feel safe. Please, God. I'll do anything. Just tell me what you want.*

She really didn't like being in her house at all anymore. She definitely didn't like going upstairs if Barney didn't want to go too. She felt safer at the office, at the mall, in her car—just about anywhere else. Even worse than the paranoia that seemed to envelop her every moment was the sadness that so much had been taken away from her that night—not just her sleep and feeling of safety but also her confidence. Confidence was the one thing she really needed to hold on to. If she had been more awake, she would have been angry about that. As it was, it was just one more thing that was gone.

Chloe was the first one to see the change in her. Chloe wasn't just her assistant; she was her best friend. She finally asked Olive if she was sick and just wasn't telling anyone. "You look like hell. I have no idea where your mind is. It's like you're not even here," she said, finally confronting her. "I just don't know how much longer I can cover for you."

She knew Chloe was right. Once, Chloe had found Olive asleep at her desk, and she often had to fix errors before emails or reports went out. They both knew that Chloe was running the department. There was an undercurrent of irritation and resentment that they both felt; hairline fractures were forming in their friendship.

Olive weighed the risks of telling her everything, anticipating the worst. At first, she really thought she had fooled everyone. Then she became too tired to care. Now she was backed into a corner. She might lose not only her job but also her best friend.

Chapter 4

Childhood Terrors

....

Maybe it was like some kind of PTSD. She felt as if everything happening to her now was like what had happened before. It was not exactly the same, but she definitely felt the same fear and the same helplessness. She figured that was why she was so on edge now—because she never really had dealt with the other experiences. Since the worst stuff always had happened during college vacations, she just never had gone back home after graduation. Then her parents had divorced, and the house had been sold. She'd thought that would end all the memories. But now she guessed not. *How do you deal with something you can't even begin to explain? Maybe I should have found a psychiatrist or something so I wouldn't be such a mess now.*

It had been fun and a little quirky in the beginning. The lights flashing on and off. The knocks that seemed to answer questions. The woman singing in the basement, who was caught on the tape recorder. The footsteps on the stairs or in the upstairs hallway. Once, she and her mother had followed the deliberate knocking on the wall behind them as it moved around the family room and ended with the rapping on the left armrest of Olive's chair. She had looked at her mother and grinned with excitement. They all had watched as a little ketchup packet slowly levitated off the kitchen table about a foot and then dropped down. "I didn't see that," her father had said. He always said that.

She even had written a story called "Split-Level Ghost" for a creative-writing class in her senior year of high school. She'd gotten a good grade on it, she recalled, but truthfully, there hadn't been much creativity involved. She'd just reported what happened. The hardest part had been deciding which of the countless happenings to include.

A new house in the suburbs didn't fit the standard pattern for a traditional haunted house, especially not in this suburb. She was sure the town council wouldn't have permitted haunted houses. She'd always had new adventures to excitedly share each morning at school. Her best girlfriends had been disappointed that nothing fun happened during sleepovers.

But then one day it hadn't been fun anymore.

She saw him for the first time as she was running down the stairs. He was halfway up the steps as she ran through him. In that split second, she saw that his clothes were dark and dirty, and he was thin and kind of tall. But it was his scowl as he looked at her, filled with anger and hatred, that frightened her the most. There was something personal about the look. It wasn't her brothers, her sister, or her parents he hated. It was her.

She saw him again a day or two later. She had a flash of him scowling right in front of her as she was washing her hair. He was maybe only a foot away. That was the last time she ever closed her eyes in the shower. Even years later, when she had her own house, she kept her eyes open. It was also the last time she took her time in getting dressed or even being naked. Until the day she moved out several years later, showers were as fast as possible. She had thought that ghosts mostly ignored the people around them. She wondered if this had been his house and if he wanted them out.

It seemed the worst things happened during the night, especially between midnight and three o'clock. Twice, she woke up in the middle of the night feeling as if she were being suffocated. She couldn't move, but she could moan loudly enough that her parents ran into her room, saving her from some unknown fate. She had an image of a pillow over her face, but of course, that wasn't possible. *Is that what they call sleep paralysis? No one ever mentioned that it felt like someone was trying to kill you.*

Then the worst thing happened. Even years later, she could feel herself helplessly going into a panic when she recalled the times when she'd had her sheet and blanket yanked beyond her feet and felt those disgusting, grotesque hands all over her body. Her arms and legs flailed at the unseen attacker; she was powerless to defend herself. She had never before felt so sickened and vulnerable, and she had never before been so frightened.

The only way to survive that summer was to wait till four or five o'clock in the morning to go to sleep. She read, watched TV, or did anything she could to focus on anything else that wasn't scary. She could still hear things, such as knocks on the walls or weird sounds, but she wasn't physically touched as long as she stayed awake. Her sewing machine in the corner of the bedroom would come alive and run by itself. A menacing chuckle seemed to come out of the walls. Sometimes there was a face in the window. But if she ignored everything and stayed awake till dawn, she could survive another night.

Whether she was awake or asleep, she figured it was safer to keep her bedroom door unlocked in case others needed to run in to save her, and even after five o'clock, when she finally collapsed from exhaustion, the bedroom light always stayed on. She counted down the days till she could return to her dorm.

Every so often, one of her brothers would talk about seeing something move or hearing a strange sound but nothing scary. It was all still fun to them. She was a little jealous; she wished it was still fun for her. If she did say anything about something scary that happened, she could see one of them giving the other an eye roll or a loud whisper that she was going crazy. Having an insane older sister was an obvious embarrassment to them. She stopped talking about the scary stuff. Everything started to build inside like a volcano getting ready to erupt, but there wasn't anything she could do about it.

Escaping back to the safety of college life was a reprieve from the continuous fear, but she still couldn't shake the feeling that she was always being watched, especially when she was alone. She and her roommate had always been pretty good friends, but Olive soon realized the constant paranoia was more than her friend wanted to deal with. Betsy was tolerant at first, but after a few weeks, it became obvious that it was more than she could take, especially when Olive tried to talk to her about all the horrible things that had happened to her over the summer. Their last conversation started with "Look, Olive, I really do care about you, but …"

She moved out in winter quarter.

Her parents told her that professional exorcists had come to the house twice. A well-known author of books about hauntings had come to investigate. "Our house is going to be in one of his next books. Isn't that exciting? It had something to do with the property, not the house. You'll feel safe the next time you come home."

She never again felt she could totally relax in that house. Maybe not anywhere. She would never again go to a Halloween haunted house, see a scary movie, read a book about ghosts, or have anything to do with dark, scary things. She would never again be able to relax, knowing there were invisible things that might hurt her. Never.

Chapter 5

Chloe

....

Olive finally had to tell somebody, or the volcano was going to blow. Chloe was the most obvious choice.

It wasn't that Chloe didn't believe her. If Olive had been making up the story, Chloe figured she could have come up with something more believable than being attacked by extraterrestrials. But she didn't exactly believe her either. She wasn't sure what to believe. What was a friend supposed to do in situations like this? She mostly tried to be supportive since Olive was convinced something had happened.

"You need to learn how to protect yourself," Chloe said emphatically. "You need to make sure these things don't happen to you anymore." She thought she had heard Oprah say something like that. Or maybe it had been Dr. Oz.

The nightmares continued but maybe not as often. She also still saw creatures, but mostly, they didn't bother her as much. Maybe she was just getting used to seeing them, or maybe she realized they didn't seem to be interested in hurting her. They weren't actually ignoring her, though, since she was pretty sure they sometimes reacted to her seeing them.

Three days of sleeping on Chloe's couch helped Olive to emerge from her stupor. She mentally added more to the growing list of ways Chloe was always there to help. It seemed obvious Olive wouldn't be able to repay her for everything in just one lifetime. Was there such a thing as an Earth angel? If so, Chloe qualified. Barney was satisfied to explore new places to sniff and sleep.

"Trust me, I've prayed my heart out every single night," Olive said. "Maybe God's upset with me. I haven't been to church since I was a kid. Maybe I'm not very good at it. I don't know. And besides, what am I protecting myself from?"

Chloe wasn't religious either but thought that prayer was probably helpful. At least it was a starting point. "Do extraterrestrials pay attention to prayers? Is there some kind of divine being who coordinates ET abductions?" She didn't know much about this stuff. She was open to the idea of ghosts and life on other planets, but her experience was limited to the movies. Olive's recent experiences didn't seem to be about ghosts, so she wondered if there were any movies about extraterrestrial kidnappings. "What about angels and all those beings from the Bible? Are they always good and helpful, or are there rogue ones that cause trouble for humans? How about the stories of evil spirits who torment people just for fun? Are they real, or are they like the Loch Ness Monster or Bigfoot?"

Chloe considered calling a priest or an exorcist. "Do they also protect from aliens, or do they just banish demons? Maybe hanging religious symbols around the house or burying crystals on the property would help. Are there people who specialize in keeping aliens away from you? Can you alien-proof your home?" She felt a little guilty when she realized there was a part of her that was intrigued by all this. Then she got a little worried when she wondered if the aliens might have followed Olive into her apartment, and she thought it might be a good idea to also protect her own place.

There were countless suggestions on the internet, but she was overwhelmed by the options. Some ideas were possibly helpful, but other ideas seemed just plain goofy. Experts talked about special prayers, the power of positive thinking, or keeping salt lamps on all day and night. Sometimes essential oils or special meditations helped. Then there were others who said it was an honor to be selected to be contacted. It was like a gift from the universe, and the chosen one was special. Maybe that was true, but Olive didn't see it that way.

Chloe offered to spend the night at Olive's house, but there was no way Olive would return home at this point. As much as she loved her friend, Chloe started to wonder how long Olive would be camped out in her apartment.

"I think you need to talk to somebody." Chloe was convinced they needed to find somebody who had experience in these things. From her internet searches, she'd learned that a lot of people were seeing UFOs and even having contacts of some kind. Sorting through websites, she found that some experiences were as frightening as Olive's had been, including reports of being kidnapped or somehow harmed. Many people talked about periods of lost time, a strange rash or burn, or memories of being in a strange place. There were stories about feeling an electrical sensation while walking through a crop circle.

Most people just wanted to talk about odd or interesting incidents that had happened to them, such as seeing something in the air that wasn't a hot-air balloon or airplane, seeing flashing bright lights, or recalling dreams about living on other planets. Some of the stories were even positive, saying the aliens almost seemed angelic. The encounters left the people feeling happy and almost encouraged about the way the world was headed. Chloe wasn't sure what an angel would look like if she saw one. What if angels didn't look like all those paintings in museums? What if angels really were the little green men?

"There's a Meetup group this evening that I think we should go to," Chloe said. "You haven't been out of my apartment in three days, and I think it's time to find some answers."

Olive was sure she would lose that argument.

Chapter 6

Starseed Connection

....

Olive looked at the twenty chairs neatly assembled in a circle and realized with dread that there wasn't a back row to hide in. Chloe was already talking to a couple who appeared to be in their fifties. A display of upcoming programs and classes was mounted on one wall—therapies for children, how to work with crystals, meditation techniques, yoga for beginners. She wasn't sure about this place, but so far, it seemed harmless enough. She figured she could fake interest for a couple of hours.

"Have you seen a UFO? Maybe had contact with someone who wasn't of this world?" was the bright red headline of one flyer. "You're not alone!" Words flew off the page at her: *safe, trust, believe,* and *understand.* The flyer explained, "Sometimes we don't feel safe telling others who don't understand and who haven't had similar experiences. It can feel lonely and isolating since you're not willing to risk ridicule. But here you will be believed, because we've had experiences too."

A man in his midtwenties was greeting the half dozen people milling about. Olive had been watching him from the safety of the literature rack and assumed he was the group's coordinator. "Hi. I'm Jason," he said, extending his hand. "Welcome to Starseed."

She mumbled a polite response and wondered once again what she could possibly have in common with everyone here. She was pretty sure no one would understand what had happened to her.

"What brings you here this evening?"

She gave another hurried, mumbled response about being with a friend who'd wanted to come. She had no interest in opening herself up to being mocked. Chairs were starting to fill with enthusiastic bodies, and Chloe motioned her over to two adjacent seats. A few minutes later, Jason went around the circle, inviting people to introduce themselves and, if they felt comfortable, share any interesting experiences they might have had.

Someone had seen a UFO when he was a child; now he was passionate about learning everything he could. The couple were there out of curiosity. One woman said she never had felt she was supposed to live on Earth; she was feeling homesick for her real family.

Only four more people until it was her turn. Olive started to mentally craft a believable answer. A young mother looked even more anxious than Olive felt, but she quietly spoke about seeing a TV program on aliens and immediately remembering that she had seen one when she was a child. A man who reminded Olive of her grandfather talked about being in the military when he was younger and how many unidentified objects he had been told to ignore. A college student talked about flashing lights that didn't move for twenty minutes over his house. He wrapped up with a laugh by saying that he hadn't been drinking or smoking anything.

All eyes then turned to Olive. "I'm just here because my friend asked me to come with her," she said. Was that really the best she could come up with? How lame was that? She supposed everyone could tell she was lying.

Chloe glanced over at her, slightly raised an eyebrow, and then talked about the research paper she was writing for her sociology class. She had always had an interest in life on other planets, so she thought this would be something she might explore for her paper.

Then the unimaginable happened. The woman almost at the end of the circle spoke haltingly, slowly measuring every word. Patricia had been on a country road a few years ago. It wasn't too late, but since it was February, it was already dark. There were strange flashing lights in the middle of the road, with an intensity that seemed to blind her. Whatever it was, it was too large to be a car or truck; she thought maybe a plane had made an emergency landing on the roadway.

As she drove closer to the lights, her car's engine suddenly died. Then the radio stopped working. The headlights went out. Words tumbled out as memories seemed to overwhelm her. She was reliving the experience. The fear she remembered also penetrated everyone in the circle.

She was aware that something was wrong. She had to get away from there. There was a high-pitched whine that seemed to surround her. She furiously tried to get the car started again to back up as fast as she could.

She considered running to get help but realized she might be safer in her car. She didn't know this road well, and she wasn't sure which way she would go. She thought about her phone in the trunk. She had thought her purse was safer back there—bad decision.

Then she saw a group of maybe five or six approaching her car. With the brilliant light behind them, she saw only dark figures coming closer. But they didn't look like any people she had seen before. They were tall, seven or eight feet, and unnaturally thin. They had long, thin arms; long, thin fingers; and heads that didn't seem to have noses or mouths. She couldn't stop staring at those huge eyes coming closer and closer.

The only place she could think to hide was on the floor of the front seat. She frantically tried to squeeze under the dash. Then the car doors all opened.

Hours later, she was in her driveway with the car engine still running. She didn't remember driving home, but she obviously had. She was exhausted, had a pounding headache, and wondered if that was what happened when someone almost fell asleep at the wheel. She hadn't felt tired when she left the restaurant at eight o'clock. She took a quick look at the dashboard clock: 12:45. That wasn't possible. It was only a twenty-minute drive from the place where she had stopped.

Memories bubbled up to the surface. She recalled the tall things with the big eyes grabbing her and taking her into the flashing lights. Some kind of a restraint. Screaming for help. She was alone in total darkness. She saw movement. Then they came back. She was in some kind of laboratory, naked. Some kind of cold machine touched her. She felt pain.

Now it was 12:45 a.m., and she had flashes of something horrific and a pounding headache. She pounded on the front door, screaming for her husband to let her in. He had been frantic; the police, the hospitals, and her girlfriends had all been called several times. He held her for a long time until she could finally talk.

Patricia paused, and everyone in the circle remained quiet long after she stopped talking. Patricia stared at her feet without expression. She assumed she wouldn't be believed even here, but she still needed to talk, to tell her story. She started shaking uncontrollably as words again poured out of her faster and faster.

Her husband asked how many drinks she had had at dinner. When he saw her blouse not buttoned correctly, he was even more convinced she was lying about the stupid UFO story, especially since the police later said they hadn't seen anything unusual in the area that night. The horrible night was even worse after the names he called her and all the screaming at her to confess the truth.

"But I saw it. It happened. I'm not lying," she said.

A second person in the group started to cry. It started with a piercing wail of countless nights filled with helplessness and terror. It held the pain of covers ripped beyond her feet. It screamed with the panic of hearing the skeleton key fall from her door and watching them get closer and closer. It shared Patricia's fear of telling others and not being believed. With each sob, Olive let Patricia and the entire circle know that she understood.

Chapter 7

The Importance of Protection

....

"I'm sorry. I'm so sorry." Olive apologized for causing a scene, looking ridiculous, and taking up too much time. She apologized for apologizing. Then Patricia told everyone how sorry she was for triggering Olive's memories. Everyone talked at once, consoling, supporting, and offering Kleenex and glasses of water.

When it was over, the turmoil almost felt cathartic. Patricia and Olive hugged each other long and hard, clutching at each other with unrestrained joy. Finally, there was someone who understood, who knew Olive wasn't crazy. The rest of the circle were also animated when they realized they now had something close to proof that each of their own experiences really had happened. If something huge, such as Patricia's and Olive's encounters really had happened—and no one doubted they had—then their own stories might also be believed, right?

Chloe, watching everything unfold with something between curiosity and awe, was no longer on the fence. Part of her felt she should apologize for having been a little bit skeptical—okay, more than just a little bit—but there were already too many apologies flying around. She could handle that later.

She often studied people, looking for details that might provide answers to behavior or personality. No one in the circle appeared to be crazy or an attention-seeker. All seemed to sincerely believe they had had an experience they didn't understand, and the pain they were feeling was palpable when they openly talked about being misunderstood. They could lose their jobs. They would be ostracized. One daughter-in-law had threatened not to let a couple see their grandchildren if they continued with the crazy stories. Now Olive was one of them. Maybe this was what it meant to have a tribe. Whatever was happening, it felt as if a roomful of strangers had just bonded.

"So what happens now?" Olive asked. "How do I just go back to life as usual? I'm still seeing horrible creatures in my dreams or sometimes when my eyes are closed for just a little bit. I've got a job and a house I need to return to—eventually." The last word wasn't lost on Chloe.

Everyone's eyes turned to Jason, as though he were keeper of the secrets. "This is just a suggestion, but the first thing you might want to do is release some of the fear you've been holding on to," he said. "Until you control the fear, the fear controls you. After that, you'll be better equipped to think about the next steps." There were general murmurs of assent and a few nods. Everyone understood what that meant. "And sometimes others can help you to get to a better place. That's what we do here."

Olive's eyes darted to the literature rack, searching for anything that might hold a clue for the next step. There were too many choices.

"You may want to start with Reiki," Jason added, and several people in the circle agreed that might be a good place to begin. "It's a Japanese technique for pain and stress relief. Very relaxing. And don't worry; you keep your clothes on."

So that's why this place is called the Center, she thought.

Olive had been stressed since the incident, but she had never told anyone about the panic attacks she had been having. But strangely, there was an odd anxiety at other times as well. She felt anxiety and such deep sadness that she sometimes felt like crying for no reason at all. She wasn't sure she wanted to talk about this with anyone yet.

The nurse at the end of the circle hadn't said a word other than during her introduction. "But how does somebody feel safe?" she asked softly. "It feels like things are happening to me that I don't understand. I seem to pick up others' bad moods. I go into places where it's like I can feel tension in the air. Sometimes I come home too exhausted to do anything but sleep. I really love my job, but sometimes being at the hospital is just so emotionally exhausting." After a pause, she continued. "It took a lot for me to come here tonight."

Someone asked her if she knew about protection, and she replied that once, she had burned so much white sage that the smoke detectors had gone off.

The man who'd seen a UFO in his backyard said she needed to learn how to create an energy boundary to protect herself at all times. "I even put one around my home, my car, and my office at work. Jeez, you can't walk down the street or go shopping without being bombarded by others' bad vibes."

"It's actually pretty easy to do, and there are lots of ways to do it," the grandmother added. "I imagine a bubble or shield of shiny white light that completely surrounds me."

Someone else talked about imagining mirrors all around her to reflect back anything she didn't want. Another person said she called on guides and angels to keep her safe, adding that she'd asked Archangel Michael to walk next to her since she was a teenager.

Jason jumped in. "How about if I lead all of us in the protection exercise we use here at the Center? You can see how easy it is to do on your own."

Everyone immediately quieted down, closed his or her eyes, and started to take long, deep breaths. Jason quietly spoke.

"Let's take a few more deep breaths. Good. Now try to feel grounded. Sometimes it helps to put your feet on the floor or imagine you have roots going from your body deep into the earth. Now imagine a tiny light in the center of your body—maybe in your solar-plexus area or heart center. Right now, it might look as small as candlelight. It might look like fire or pure white light—whatever you choose. It may be small now, but know that this is your power, your personal power, and we're going to use it to protect you. See it come from deep inside you.

"Now use your willpower to visualize the energy of this light get stronger, get larger, and start to fill up your body. The light is expanding into your chest, throat, and head and down your shoulders to your fingertips. The light is moving down into your stomach, hips, and legs and all the way to your toes. Everything that this light touches that isn't good for you, it cleanses. It purifies. Or the negative energy moves outside of your energy field so that it can't bother you anymore. See yourself completely filled with this amazingly powerful light.

"Now, because your skin is only an artificial boundary, imagine that this light is so powerful that it explodes outside your body, and you are now standing inside a protective ball of light. It might be out a couple feet or just a few inches, but see if you can feel this light protect you from anything you don't need. Let the energy decide if something needs to be sent away. You don't need to even worry what it might be.

"Now, if you want to, you can put something else on the outside of this bubble to make it even more protective. Maybe it's armor or titanium so that nothing can get through that isn't for your greatest good. Or something slippery so that something you don't want near you can just slide off. Or, since nobody knows what you're doing, maybe you see dragons patrolling the border. This one is totally your call.

"Now take a good look at the final image you just created. Remember this image, because you will want to immediately recall it. Now slowly bring your awareness back in the room."

Some opened their eyes right away, wiggling fingers and stretching a bit. Others took longer, as though they were kittens coming out of a relaxing nap.

"So that took about two minutes. How does everyone feel? Good? Good." Jason scanned the room for nodding heads. "After you imagine the light protecting you, you can even push it out farther to fill the room you're in and even your whole house. It works.

"But here's another thing to think about: We all know that sometimes you don't always have two minutes to build your fire. Maybe somebody's walking up to you who is angry about something, or you're in a meeting, and you feel like you need extra armor. What you can use is something we call the *airbag technique*. You all still remember that final image, right? So believe that you have the ability to go to that final image in a heartbeat. In a second. Think about how fast an airbag opens up to save your life, and imagine that your light can come out that fast to surround you with energetic protection."

It only took one practice for everyone to feel safer, even the nurse.

Olive and Chloe looked at each other and both realized that something had changed. They weren't sure what it was yet, but they thought they might have found a tribe.

As she was driving home, Olive felt her familiar confidence returning. "I'm going home tomorrow night. Barney and me." She was staring straight ahead in the car, as though she were determined to see the future. "I can't even begin to tell you how much I appreciate all your help, even suggesting that we go there tonight. But he was right. I have been letting fear control me. I can do this."

Chloe nodded in encouragement. She wasn't sure Olive's new tribe was her tribe too. After all, she hadn't had any of the experiences the others had had. She thought she might try attending the group one more time just to keep Olive company, but it didn't seem like her thing. Actually, she wasn't sure what her thing was. But they all seemed nice enough, and it had been pretty interesting to hear everyone's stories. Just in case aliens had followed Olive to her apartment, Chloe thought she'd better use the technique to keep them out. Maybe she would create two or three more layers of protection just in case—definitely dragons on the outer layer.

When they got home, they agreed it might be a good idea to sit quietly in the living room to practice protecting themselves and the apartment. Olive took Jason's suggestion and watched the tiny flicker of candlelight grow into a powerful bonfire. Interestingly, she actually felt a little warmer when she was done. She liked this exercise for a couple of reasons. First of all, it was easy to remember. Plus, it gave her something to do to make herself feel more in charge of her life and less like a victim. What had he said? "If you don't control the fear, the fear will control you."

A series of memories appeared in her mind, showing too many times when she had felt powerless, even going back to childhood, as though she hadn't had any control over what happened to her. Or maybe it was a feeling that she didn't deserve to have that kind of power. She recalled with surprise that the feeling had been there long before the scary experiences on college breaks at her parents' house. *Have I been acting like a victim all my life? Is that why scary things happen to me and not to other people?* That was definitely going to change.

When she came out of the meditation, Chloe was already getting ready for bed. Olive supposed it took her friend less time to create her fire. Or maybe she did the airbag technique.

Olive was starting to look forward to going back to work. She missed her house. She missed the Olive she used to be. She thought the old Olive might be coming back now. She fell asleep watching another protective bonfire fill her room.

The next day, Olive threw herself into work with an enthusiasm she hadn't felt in a long time. The in-box was pretty empty, thanks to Chloe, but she let out a long sigh when she saw the massive pile marked "For your attention." She made a note to bring in flowers tomorrow morning. If not for Barney, she could easily have worked late into the night, but she still needed to pick up dinner for both of them.

There was a brief flicker of anxiety around bedtime, but otherwise, she didn't notice anything out of the ordinary. Maybe tomorrow night, she would experiment with turning some of the lights off.

The night was mostly uneventful, especially with the protective-energy bonfire around the house. She remembered waking up once with a feeling of anxiety and perhaps hearing someone cry. It sounded like a child. Barney's soft snoring felt reassuring. Otherwise, it didn't seem anything was troubling in the bedroom. *Probably just a dream.* She rolled over and fell back asleep.

Chapter 8

Artie

....

Olive considered attending the next Starseed meeting. She was curious about what might happen this time, and she had to admit it was a little exciting to step into something that seemed almost taboo. The scariness of weeks ago was fading, and nothing bad had happened since she returned to her house. She felt confident she could talk about her scary experiences without throwing up.

But the next session wasn't scheduled for another two weeks, and she didn't want to be at a disadvantage for this meeting too. It bugged her when she was drawn into a conversation about something she knew nothing about. She prided herself on having just enough information about just enough things that she could fake just about anything. But there were mentions of topics she had always considered New Age mumbo jumbo, such as crystals or spirit guides. But they mostly seemed like normal people; she couldn't understand why they would believe such silliness. Understanding their odd belief systems wasn't required for going to the meeting, but she thought it might be helpful to do a little studying in preparation.

She could be a bit obsessive about learning, preferring to read histories rather than romance novels. She didn't see the purpose in watching sitcoms and had no interest in doing anything that wasted her time. She knew how driven she could be at times; actually, she told herself that was one of her most endearing characteristics. She supposed there were others who instead

29

saw it as irritating, but right now, she didn't care. She wanted information or a therapy session or maybe just to talk to the woman she had connected with at the meeting. She grabbed her laptop and claimed an empty table in the corner coffee shop.

She wasn't sure where to start. Someone in the meeting had handed her a black rock when she was crying. It could have been her imagination, but she was pretty sure she'd felt better after that. She started searching for black rocks. *Black tourmaline, jet, onyx, hematite. Good grief,* she thought. *How is anybody supposed to know what they are all for? Obsidian, black quartz, black amethyst.*

The stones all looked the same on her laptop. Supposedly, some were for grounding, keeping one focused, helping to manifest, removing negativity, and cleansing. Some transformed heavier energies into lighter energies. She wondered who had figured all this out.

Some of them helped to heal physical issues; some worked on emotions. One helped with protection, took away fears, and made a person feel safer. She thought she had better buy a bunch of those. One helped with spiritual development. She wondered what religion had to do with it.

Her sigh must have been louder than she'd thought. "I like black tourmaline," said a voice behind her. Someone was looking over her shoulder. "But I have a lot of hematite too." If he noticed her glare, he didn't acknowledge it. "It mostly depends on how you want to use it. What are you thinking?" He pointed to one of the online images and said, "Beautiful. Isn't that just beautiful?"

She prided herself on her glare: firm but not rude, with eyes closed just a bit and with a neutral expression, communicating displeasure with professionalism. Her staff knew exactly what she was thinking without her needing to say a word. Chloe once had told her that her team called it *the look* behind her back. Crystal Guy would receive the full fury of the look when he finally took his eyes off the screen.

"Oh, sorry," he said. "I'm Artie. I just wondered if I could help."

She was incredulous. He had completely ignored the look. *No one ignores the look.* She surveyed him for a quick moment and then said she didn't know much about rocks. "I was with some people a while ago who seemed to be into them, and I was trying to figure out why."

"I'm no expert, but I can tell you what little I know," he answered. "Can I get you a coffee?"

"Decaf cappuccino." She realized she'd just invited him to her table. It had been a while since she'd had someone steady in her life, and she kicked herself for being so out of practice.

She got a better look as he was ordering their drinks. He looked about her age, maybe a little older, and was around five foot seven, which was about four inches taller than she was. He had salt-and-pepper hair and was cute. She wasn't interested in anything more than a cup of coffee with a cute stranger, but it would pass an hour or so and maybe give her a little practice if she ever decided to date again.

She thanked him for the cappuccino and decided to drop the look, especially since it hadn't worked. She told him her name was Olive Stuart, she was thirty-two, and she was a program director for a community center. She loved her job, her team, and the shaggy roommate she'd found at a nearby shelter. At some point, she realized he was really paying attention to her and even asking questions, not like the last one.

The overhead lights were turned off in a not-so-subtle hint that the coffee shop had closed. It had been four hours, and they hadn't discussed black crystals.

Chapter 9

Spirituality versus Religion

....

"Again? Haven't you seen him like every night this week?" Chloe asked. At first, she had said she was happy for Olive, but lately, there was an unmistakable edge to her voice. After all, they hadn't done much together in the past few weeks.

But in all fairness, Olive thought, Chloe now turned down every offer of lunch. *What's up with that?* Olive thought she sounded a bit jealous. If so, that wasn't fair, especially since Olive had lived through the details of every one of Chloe's dates.

But then Olive's thoughts usually turned to Artie. There was something different about him that Olive found intriguing and even puzzling. He knew everything about cars, especially race cars; was an avid golfer; and followed the local pro hockey team. He definitely followed the macho playbook. But he had suggested going to a psychic fair for their first date and then afterward watching an opera on TV with a bottle of red wine. It was the most memorable first date ever. He loved modern dance and had season tickets to the ballet. And he was interested in rocks. "No, these here are usually called crystals," he often reminded her.

She told him about the dead-of-night experiences, both recently and when she was a teenager. She also disclosed what she could almost remember from when she was about five. She was rewarded with a long hug and his telling her he would have protected her. She wasn't sure how he could have fended off the monsters, but she believed him nevertheless. She even told him that for some reason, she lately was starting to feel anxious for no apparent reason and sometimes even had panic attacks. They both knew that someday he would get the chance to keep her safe all night long. If he was going to protect her from the bogeyman, they both agreed he probably should join her at Starseed meetings. This seemed like the best place for accurate information.

It wasn't a surprise that Chloe passed on attending future Starseed classes. She was the best administrative assistant anyone could ever have had, but with as grouchy as Chloe had been lately, it was okay with Olive that she didn't go. Her best friend was becoming more distant. She was still doing her work but not really herself. Olive saw long periods of spaciness, as if her friend couldn't focus, or she didn't even look like she wanted to. Considering how much Chloe had protected her a few months ago, Olive thought she would give her some time to work through whatever she needed to. That was what friends did.

But after several weeks, things still weren't improving. In fact, they seemed to be getting worse. Chloe had taken up smoking cigarettes and maybe other things as well and took frequent breaks to the back garden. They used to share fun things they saw on Facebook, but recently, Chloe said she almost never looked at it anymore. One day she even showed up in the same outfit she'd had on the day before. When Olive asked if she was okay, she snapped at her and told her to leave her alone. That had never happened before. Their relationship was changing. Yelling at a friend was one thing, but yelling at one's boss was problematic.

Olive thought she must not have been doing a good job of explaining her concerns to the HR director, because Rob didn't seem to understand at all. "I'm really sorry, Olive," he said, "but I don't think anyone here has seen anything different. At least I haven't. We see her up here a lot, and she's just as bubbly and helpful as she's always been. But you might want to keep a careful record of all of your observations, just in case something needs to be addressed at some point."

The log had been started weeks ago. *But how do you prove something when it only seems to happen around you?*

But then others on her team also started to see changes. It was as though Chloe's entire personality were shifting. Actually, she seemed to flip back and forth from the old Chloe to whatever this new version was. The change could be quick. It was as though something could take over in the blink of an eye. In reality, sometimes it seemed her eyes really did change. Sometimes they looked cold and dead. Sometimes angry. Sometimes her whole face could look almost hateful. When someone asked her what time she needed to leave for an appointment, Chloe answered, "She needs to leave at noon." There was a stunned pause while everyone absorbed what she had said. *She?*

The oddest part was the unpredictability. Sometimes she was smiling, cracking jokes, and being her old self. Those were the best times, when they still worked together as the perfect team. But no one knew how long those times would last or when the new Chloe would emerge from the depths of some personal hell. Everyone, including Olive, started to avoid her, leaving messages in Chloe's mailbox or sending emails rather than taking a chance on finding her in darkness.

Once, when Chloe was in one of her good moods, Olive asked her if she knew she seemed to sometimes have a different personality. Yeah, she knew, she said, but she couldn't seem to control it. Sometimes she could feel herself start to get angry or depressed, and then it was as if she just faded away, and something else came out. "That doctor's appointment last week? It was with a psychiatrist, but after I drove to his office, it was as though I just forgot to go inside. I don't know what to do. Last week, I started cutting," she said as she showed her left arm to her horrified boss. She said it was okay for Olive to drive her to the next appointment to make sure she actually went inside.

Chloe wondered if depression could come on that quickly. If so, how was it possible to switch so rapidly between being normal and being depressed? She had no idea. How about bipolar disorder or schizophrenia? How did one get something called a dissociative disorder? There was no doubt: it was almost as though there were two different people in her. The old Chloe was mostly vegetarian; the new one seemed to live on hamburgers. The old Chloe loved to experiment with hair clips and styling her long hair; the new one barely brushed hers. Olive had to face the reality that the Chloe she had loved to be with just wasn't around as much anymore.

Two of her staff asked for a confidential meeting. The older of the two said that she had seen something like that happen with someone in her family. "It was weird," she said. "I don't know what he was into, but his whole personality was different. We all thought it was probably drugs. He ended up killing himself."

"Maybe there really is someone else in there too," the other one said. "Maybe she needs an exorcism. I saw a YouTube video once, and it's actually a lot more common than people know. I wonder if it's contagious."

Olive immediately replied that there was no need to be ridiculous, but she still made a mental note to research demonic possession. She was in foreign territory now. She suspected exorcisms probably weren't covered by their health savings account.

Date nights with Artie meant they had become regular visitors at the Center, often trying different sessions or even the same modality at the same time and then sharing experiences afterward. Or they would take turns selecting a class on something that sounded interesting. Crystals had brought them together, but their new interest in exploring a whole new world kept them wanting more.

Spirituality was the hardest concept for Olive to grasp, as she had always been taught that it was the same thing as religion. Everything at the Center was supposed to be open to all faiths, but she wasn't sure how to differentiate between the two concepts, and she had an even more difficult time in reconciling the beliefs she had developed her entire life with what she was now experiencing for herself. Part of her felt guilty for enjoying what her parents would have forbidden.

She had attended Sunday school when she was young and knew all about the stories and what her parents believed. She could lead grace at the dinner table and even recite some Bible verses. But at some point, maybe around age twelve, something in the weekly church services hadn't felt right for her anymore. Hymns written hundreds of years ago didn't make sense. She wondered why a loving God allowed all the wars and injustice in the world. Couldn't he just tell everyone to stop it? Sometimes it seemed as if keeping one's shoes shiny was more important than paying attention to the speakers. And why was it that so many religions basically believed the same thing, yet nobody got along? Nothing made sense. Her uncle, who went to church all the time, was upset at her when she gave him a clay cross she had made in art class, and he said loudly, "That's not my cross!"

She knew it didn't look exactly like the ones in his church, but she hadn't realized until then how much of a mistake she had made.

There was much she didn't understand about what her parents said were the right beliefs and which were the wrong ones. Some of the people she cared about had the wrong beliefs, even though they were the nicest people she knew. She wondered if they knew they were going to hell. Some of the people she knew who talked about God, Jesus, and heaven all the time didn't seem like nice people underneath the smiles. She often asked her mother why she wasn't supposed to like people who didn't look like her or went to a different church. "They're not like us" put an end to those discussions.

When she was old enough to stay home alone, she stopped going to church. This first act of independence included a lot of yelling, and her father said she was embarrassing the whole family. Her younger brothers and sister still didn't have a choice, and they often looked wistfully at Olive grinning at them in her pajamas as they left. When everyone returned hours later, her aunt reassured her that she had said a prayer for Olive's soul and that her uncle had put an extra dollar in the collection plate to make sure she was saved. She thanked them, but that always made her feel like she must have been a bad person. What about everyone else who didn't go to that church? Did they also feel like bad people? Nothing about religion made sense to her; she just knew it made her feel sad.

She would occasionally go to a church when someone got married or if she was exploring a historic area of a city, but she didn't see the need to put much emotional energy into it. Now here she was, trying to understand that spirituality wasn't the same thing as religion after all.

"Every single one of us is connected to Source," the teacher explained. "Some people call this God, Spirit, the divine, or Allah. It's not really important what you call it. It's that connection you were born with to experience joy, meaning, and purpose in your life. Some people find that connection through nature, art, or meditation. Some people like to have more structure in their lives—maybe in a building, such as a church or synagogue. That structure—the building, the hymnals, the preacher—is what is often called religion."

Olive still didn't understand. "But doesn't God only talk to you in church?"

Several people turned around to look at her, perhaps wondering who had asked such a naive question.

"God talks to you and you and you," the teacher said, looking around the room, "every day in countless ways. Some people hear God in the chirping of birds, a baby's cry, or a magnificent sunset or when you meditate or pray. Our biggest challenge is quieting our minds long enough to hear."

She was in deep concentration as she and Artie drove home, thinking about all the times when she had been told by her family that she was born in sin, lived in sin, and would die in sin. Never being good enough was a regular theme in her family, because that was what life was about. The fact that spirituality wasn't the same thing as religion was especially mystifying, especially the parts about spirituality's being joy, meaning, and purpose in one's life and about religion's being just one of the ways to find happiness.

"So I'm not a bad person?" she asked.

Artie reached for her hand. "You never were."

Chapter 10

Spirit Releasements

....

Over the months, Olive experimented with a number of services at the Center but avoided trying Reiki. A little voice inside her—actually, it sounded like her mother—often warned her that only the pastors of her church were qualified to do healing work; it was dangerous to let anyone else do it. She wasn't sure why that was, especially since Jesus had said that everyone could do what he did. For some reason, it also was dangerous to meditate, do yoga, or do anything else considered Eastern. *But Jesus was Middle Eastern, right?* After the discussion on religion and spirituality the other night, she suspected this might be yet another thing she had been told that wasn't true. She didn't blame her parents for keeping her away from things they thought were unsafe; they were only believing the things they had been told by their parents. She wondered how many generations before them also had believed things that weren't so. At least some of the baffling untruths would stop with her.

She had heard that Reiki was good for stress relief and anxiety, but she wasn't sure how much she believed all the hype. She had read articles about how many hospitals used it and how many people talked about how they had benefited from it, but it seemed a little too good to be true. She didn't understand how just using your hands could give you energy, make you relax, and help you focus yet make you feel all floaty. Sometimes her father's voice joined her mother's in her head to tell her to stay away.

But the panic attacks were still occasionally happening, almost always when she was alone at home. Fortunately, the anxiety was under control now that she had medication. Still, she wished she felt better. She mostly didn't understand the sadness, especially now that she and Artie were hanging out more often. She would have thought all the loneliness would have been gone by now. She ignored her parents' mental warnings and made an appointment with the Center's director.

"How did you like the talk on spirituality?" Catharine asked, recognizing Olive from the recent class.

Olive explained that a lot of the beliefs she had been raised with were being challenged, which was okay with her.

"We do that a lot around here," Catharine replied. "Actually, our primary goal is to help you discover how to empower yourself. That's why we have so many ways to help you find out who you are. That helps you to understand where you're going." Despite Olive's composure, Catharine could feel how anxious she was; it seemed her anxiety was more than first-time jitters.

"I don't know much about Reiki, but I guess I'm afraid of what might happen. I had some scary things happen to me a while ago, and I don't know that I like the idea of invisible things being in the room with us." She had heard that sometimes spirit guides or even people she had known who had died might show up.

The director nodded. "I completely understand. That can be a little confusing when you first experience helpers. Were you ever told when you were a child that you had a guardian angel?"

"Of course. But they aren't real."

"Actually, they are. Everyone who is born on Earth has a spirit companion who comes with him or her. Kind of like the buddy system. And that guide helps you to remember where you put your keys or reminds you of something, like the name of the person you're talking to. Sometimes they help us to make decisions. When we suddenly remember something or get a creative idea, we often call it women's intuition, a hunch, or gut instinct. But I always give thanks to the helpers." A loud crack came from somewhere overhead. "See? That's probably one of yours checking in on you."

A puzzled look crossed Olive's face when she was asked if she believed in reincarnation. "I never really thought about it," she replied. "I'm having enough trouble with this lifetime. I'm not sure I want to have to deal with others."

"If you want to explore the possibility, every one of us here believes that we have lived before. If you've heard of quantum physics, you know that everything is energy. Everything. Even the soul. So when we don't have these bodies anymore, the soul just moves into a different kind of energy, and then it returns when it wants to continue its growth. Sometimes I see myself like a tulip coming back every spring. The guides we work with are pure energy, whether they are an angel, your favorite uncle, or a multidimensional being. Don't worry," she said, seeing a worried expression. "We only work with the most positive and loving helpers. We always ask for your highest and greatest good."

Olive did a quick scan of the studio. The room was set up to provide a relaxing experience, with low lights, soft music, and a few candles. She lay down on the massage table and listened to a general explanation of how gentle touch would help to locate and release areas of blocked energy.

"Many people get so relaxed that they even fall asleep." Catharine suggested Olive might want to close her eyes to have a more relaxing experience.

"But why would my energy get blocked in the first place?"

"Good question," Catharine replied. "Chi, or *ki*, the Japanese word for energy, travels through the body in invisible pathways called meridians. These channels can often get blocked by emotions we aren't dealing with or sometimes due to physical trauma, like a broken bone. When that happens, we say that dis-ease can occur. An acupuncturist uses a needle that is finer than a human hair and pliable like a cat's whisker to open up the blockages in the pathways. We just use energy coming through our hands."

Trust had always been an issue for Olive, especially trusting somebody she didn't know well. Now she was being asked to also keep her eyes closed. It took a little while for Olive to realize her body was actually unwinding from the stress of the past few months. Then she felt the warmth starting to slowly build in the practitioner's hands and travel through her body. A gentle vibration buzzed in her fingers and toes. The tingling wasn't unpleasant, but it felt a little strange at first. Her right leg bounced a little once and then a second time. Catharine explained that blockages were being energetically cleared in these areas. Skeptics were always her favorite clients; she loved to see the moment when they realized it was all real. Olive was starting to feel a little sleepy and had a slight smile on her lips. More twitches came from both legs and arms.

After a half hour or so, Olive started to breathe a little heavier and occasionally pushed the practitioner's hands away. A little frown formed on her brow, and her lower lip looked as if she were pouting. She repeatedly said, "No, no, no. Go away," in a small voice.

Interesting. Catharine had seen this before and had a pretty good idea of what was coming. "What are you experiencing?" she asked.

Olive furrowed her brow and asked if it was normal to see things.

"It's actually pretty common. Sometimes memories come up that need to be released, even from childhood or events your conscious mind may have forgotten. Or you might see people or pets who have crossed over. Sometimes it's colors or shapes. Everyone has a different experience."

"Okay. I see this little girl in my mind," she answered. "She looks about eight or ten, and she's crying. I don't know who it is."

Catharine told her that she saw her too. "Many practitioners are intuitively connected to their clients during the session." She then asked Olive if it was okay with her if she talked to the little girl.

"Sure," Olive replied. Olive immediately started pleading, "I don't want to go. I don't want to go. Don't make me go. They'll be mad at me."

"Who would be mad at you?"

The little girl tried to explain in bursts of emotion: playing where she wasn't supposed to be, getting hurt, and not being able to move. Her mother would be really upset.

"Honey, no one will be angry with you," Catharine said. "They miss you and want you to be with them. Your mommy wants you to come to her." It took several minutes to convince her that she really was missed and wouldn't be punished. "You think you can't stand up because you got hurt, but you really can. Try it."

A slightly surprised look appeared on Olive's face.

"Good. Now I'm going to ask that a beautiful light come down to find you. It may look like sunshine. And I'm going to ask that all of the highest helpers please guide this little one into the light so she can find peace." Both Catharine and Olive watched as a soft beam of light started to form overhead.

Suddenly, Olive gasped loudly. "I see a woman in the light. She's coming closer. The little girl is running. She just jumped into her arms. They're both heading into the light. The light is gone now." Olive's entire body relaxed into the table.

"What just happened?" Olive stammered after the session had ended, collapsing into a chair. "That was the most amazing thing I've ever experienced. Did I imagine everything?"

"Nope, it was real. You just helped a little girl reunite with her mother. Nice job," Catharine replied. "What you had is called a releasement."

"But it was like I could feel her pain. I could really feel it. I never told anyone I had been having pain down this leg. That little girl's leg really hurt, but mostly, she was terrified. She felt alone and terrified. And more than anything, she felt like she was in big trouble."

Catharine nodded.

"And when she saw her mother ..." Olive's voice trailed off as she became emotional. "There was so much joy. Both of them. That was so beautiful."

Olive asked who the little girl was. The director told her that she didn't know but that helping people's souls move into the light was standard practice at the Center.

Olive was thoughtful. "I heard her crying once in the middle of the night, but I guess I thought it was a dream. Was she dead?"

"Yes, she was, but she was afraid to move to the light." Catharine explained that at the moment of death, moving to the light—or heaven or the other side or whatever one called it— was a choice. Not everyone did it.

"Why not?"

"There are a number of reasons. Some don't feel worthy. They say, 'Only the best people can go to heaven, and I'm not good enough.' Or they say, 'There's something I have to do. I have unfinished business. I'm the only one who can take care of my children. No one else knows where the will is hidden.' Or 'I don't want to leave all my possessions. I spent a lifetime accumulating all these things, and I'm not leaving them now.'

"Some say, 'I have a mental illness. I see a light, but I'm not sure what to do next,' or 'I have addictions, and I'm pretty sure I can't get cigarettes or alcohol or drugs up there.' Or 'I have been abused my whole life, and I don't want to take the chance that my tormenter is up there.' Or maybe

'I just committed suicide, or I'm depressed, and I'm positive that others don't want to be around me.'

"Some might say, 'Someone begged me to stay just as I was getting ready to move into the light. I would feel guilty if I left.' Or 'I'm a child, and I just don't feel like it. Nobody tells me what to do.'

"Some say, 'I had a stroke or sudden accident, and I don't realize I'm dead,' or 'I was killed, and I want revenge on the person who killed me.' Or maybe 'I've been told my whole life that I am a sinner going to hell. When I die, God is going to punish me. I saw the light and didn't want to take the chance.'"

Olive looked stricken. "Are there a lot of people who feel like that?"

"Unfortunately, yes. That's why it's so important to feel as empowered and joyful as possible. Not just for the final moment but for all moments."

"So what happens to the people who don't go to heaven?"

Catharine told her that in her experience, there were three possible choices. "Your soul goes to where it feels the most comfortable. Sometimes it's the upstairs bedroom where you spent all your time when you were alive. That's what we call a ghost. Sometimes you're homeless, or you're not connected to a special place when you die, so your soul just wanders. That's what we call an earthbound spirit. And sometimes you just want to feel safe and cared for, especially if you didn't have that in life. When this is the case, someone's soul can merge into another person's body. That is known as a spirit attachment, which is what you had. The little girl just wanted a place to feel safe."

"But it was like I was actually experiencing her sadness, like it was my sadness. I've been feeling this every day since I had a rough time months ago. So that was really her sadness? Were the panic attacks I've been having really her panic attacks? And that pain in my leg? It's gone. It's completely gone. Was that really her pain?"

"Probably," Catharine answered, "since no other entities were identified."

Olive's eyes grew wide.

Catharine explained that it was common to have more than one. "It's as if the first one holds the door open for others to come in to also feel safe."

"But how do you get one in the first place?" Her eyes were locked on the director's with an energy that said the skeptic was moving to believer.

Catharine explained. "Think about all the ways I just talked about that said, 'I'm not good enough. I'll never be good enough. I have addictions;

I'm angry or depressed.' Now imagine that right now, your energy is about here," she said, motioning to around heart level, "and their energy level is way down there," she said, pointing at the ground. "When you surround yourself with unhealthy thinking or actions, when you live in a belief that you're not good enough, or when you're under the influence or maybe really sick, where do you suppose your energy is?"

Olive pointed to the ground and nodded as the awareness grew.

"Right. So when your energies become as low as the souls who believe they are worthless, you have limited resistance. It's like how we more easily get a cold or the flu if we don't get enough sleep. Or how you can get an infection if you don't bandage a cut or open sore. Same thing."

"But why did I feel her sadness and her panic?" She needed to convince Catharine that she really could feel the little girl's pain. That it wasn't her imagination.

Catharine replied, "Because when others attach to your energy field, it's common that they also share their memories, their beliefs, and their preferences. Their sleep schedule now is your schedule. If they want to smoke or drink, you may start to smoke or drink. You could be in a great mood one day and then miserably unhappy the next if you have picked up a depressed spirit. You might start to use words you didn't use before. Heck, I've seen sweet little old ladies swear up a storm!"

She continued. "It's all energy. Keep in mind that attachments only feel comfortable in low-energy environments, which means they'll do everything they can to also keep you in low energy. It doesn't feel good for them when you're happy, so they may try to keep you away from people or situations that are positive. Sometimes they'll make sure you're distant from friends or may pick fights to make sure others don't want to be with you. They can even prevent you from getting help if you know something is wrong."

"Like a psychiatrist?" The dots were starting to connect for Olive.

Catharine wasn't sure where Olive was going with this question but agreed. "They could also say things that don't make sense, like referring to themselves as *we*."

"Or *she*," Olive added.

"Right. That's why you possibly acted differently. It's very possible your anxiety and panic attacks weren't really yours. You might feel different now."

Olive was thoughtful as she replied that she already did.

"Attached spirits are very real. I'm told that every culture and every religion has a technique for releasing them. Some people use prayer or ask archangels to help. Some people go to shamans. But realize that not everybody knows how to do this work or even wants to. We have a lot of people who come in to buy white sage or incense to clear their houses of spirits, but I don't recommend that. It takes a little more powerful mojo to help relocate souls to their new home. Just ask us to do a house-clearing for you."

"But aren't there also really bad ones? The ones we call demons or devils?"

"Yes, there are really bad ones, the ones we have to do exorcisms on to release, but the chance of you ever seeing something really bad is pretty slim. You really don't need to worry about that. One final thing," Catharine added, "and this is important to keep in mind. Ninety-nine percent of souls who choose not to go into the light are not bad people. They're sad, they're lonely, and they truly believe they aren't good enough to go to heaven. They're a grandma who didn't go to church as often as she thought she should. They're the paper boy who stepped off the curb into traffic. And they're eight-year-old girls who are afraid they'll be punished after they got hurt."

Olive gave Catharine a heartfelt hug and told her she felt better than she had in ages. "I've got a friend who needs to come here."

Chapter 11

Soon Arrive

....

Life had been pretty hectic for the past year. Olive often caught herself reliving every detail, starting with the perfect wedding: ideal weather, a simple ceremony next to the fountain in the park, and the ones they loved most. Nothing about it was traditional. Artie was dressed all in white, and Olive wore the brightest orange, yellow, and magenta dress she could find. On their way to the honeymoon suite, the other couple in the elevator stared at Olive's matching too-high magenta heels, and Artie realized they probably thought he had rented his companion by the hour. That was okay because he thought she looked mighty fine.

Even the reception was unlike anything anyone had ever seen, but it was perfect for them. The caricaturist who had drawn their wedding invitations drew large portraits of everyone attending, and the snow-cone machine offered root beer schnapps or something else equally alcoholic. Balloons and flowers were everywhere. *Wow, what an evening.*

Every photo showed Chloe grinning and making a different funny face, even in the bridal party photos. The long purple feather in her hair swung wildly as she danced. Ever since Chloe's appointment at the Center and the amazing releasement experience she had had, she was back to herself. In fact, it seemed she celebrated every chance she could.

Unbelievable, thought Olive. *What happens to people who don't get the kind of help we did?*

Of course, they both understood how weird their experiences sounded when they tried to explain, so they mostly avoided sharing details.

Life settled into comfortable predictability. Barney was probably snoring on a cloud those days. Then Molly had been with them for far too short a time, followed by two shaggy shelter dogs who now had the run of the house. Life was good.

A couple of days after New Year's Day, Olive told Chloe about the weird wind sound she'd heard, followed by the message "It's time." Neither of them gave it much thought, until it happened again while they were at work a few months later. This time, Chloe heard the sound too, along with all the others. But only Olive heard the message.

Chloe had had so many of her own interesting experiences lately, including releasing her own attached spirit, that she no longer ridiculed or was afraid of things she didn't understand. She thought it was especially interesting that almost every night at 3:00 a.m., she was wide awake. At first, she thought maybe someone got home from work at that time every night and was banging a car door, waking her up. She wasn't worried or upset but thought it was a little strange. "It happened again last night," she would tell Olive the next morning. "It's the oddest thing, but it's almost like someone is trying to talk to me. And it's always around the same time."

True to his word, Artie was the ideal protector. More than anything, it was nice to have someone in her life who enjoyed being spontaneous and who was like her but, in many other ways, different. She felt as if she had found balance in every part of her life.

"Hey, Chloe, can you come in here?" Olive yelled through the open office door. "Look at this!" Olive's hand was moving across a sheet of white paper, making sweeping and looping motions.

Chloe arched an eyebrow, not seeing the purpose of having been summoned.

"I'm not doing this. No, really. My hand is moving all by itself."

"Why?"

"Beats me. I started to write a memo, and instead, the pen began moving on its own. Weird, huh?"

The wide motions began to take shape with smaller movements and, eventually, what looked like words. The word *soon* appeared on the page and then *arrive*. The writing was slow and deliberate, with the lettering perfectly formed: *Soon arrive.*

"So if you aren't doing that, then who is?" As soon as Chloe said that, they both froze. Maybe she had another spirit attachment. In the past year, Olive, Artie, and Chloe had all taken Reiki classes, so Chloe immediately protected herself and checked Olive for wayward entities. "Nope, you're clear," she proclaimed with obvious relief. They had all decided the benefits of learning how to do Reiki the original way would pay off, even if it took a little longer. It seemed this was one of those times.

Soon arrive. It's time. Soon arrive. Olive wondered what it all meant. Sometimes it felt as if there were some kind of plan or purpose for all the experiences she had had. She wondered if these odd occurrences were somehow happening for a reason.

Chapter 12

Avratar

....

It seemed that almost every morning, something odd would pop into Olive's head just as she was waking up. Sometimes it was part of a song or maybe a word. Once in a while, she might see a face, such as the time she saw her mother looking at her with a loving smile. It was definitely her, but she looked younger, the way Olive remembered her from childhood. But she hadn't thought about her mother in ages, and if one could choose his or her guides, her mother definitely would not have been one of them.

Her mother had been gone for several years now, and Olive often saw her intuitively through her third eye. It seemed she thought of her when she made a decision or had a realization about something. Every so often, she smelled her mother's distinctive perfume. Olive had hated that perfume when she was growing up, but now she thought her mom had created the perfect way to announce she was nearby. There was no way Olive would have made that up.

But her mother as a guide? That didn't seem possible. Her mother had been judgmental and often unkind. They hadn't even been that close when she was alive, but the woman looking at her during meditations or as she was waking up radiated pure love. Then Olive learned that sometimes your best friend on the other side would volunteer to incarnate with you to help you learn the most challenging lessons. She now had to consider that the biggest thorn in one's side on this side could possibly be his or her best friend in heaven.

She considered the irony of her mother possibly being one of her helpers. When alive, her mother had been clear: one should only connect with God, Jesus, or angels and nothing else. She wondered how her mother felt about all of this now. Had she really believed that guides were wrong when she was down on earth, or had that just been part of the script she was supposed to follow in this lifetime?

The idea of guides was often confusing, but it felt like a real possibility.

She was still working on finding out about her other guides. She had some animal totems and every so often felt something in a meditation. Knocks were pretty common now, especially when she started to meditate, and every so often, there was a cool breeze. It was okay with her that her awareness of guides was gradual. *What is it that you are supposed to say? Oh yeah: "In a way I can handle."* That definitely seemed to be the way she was working with them.

Olive was also starting to be pretty good at using the pendulum. There were a few times when she forgot to discern whom she was talking to and picked up an earthbound walking through. As soon as the answers didn't make sense and she realized she'd forgotten to use the protocol, she immediately started over. She was getting better at feeling the energy of different guides, as well as why they were offering their help. One was especially good at relaxing her when she got a little tense, and another one once helped her find her missing phone. She made a point of thanking all of them every night as she was falling asleep, along with sending out her protection over both Artie and herself. Life was good.

She wasn't surprised when she woke up hearing words softly whispered inside her brain. What did surprise her was what they said: "Soon arrive." She got a little flutter in the pit of her stomach when she thought about the message. Why were they telling her they were coming, and what, if anything, was she supposed to do about it?

Artie suggested Olive take the leap from studying Reiki and getting regular sessions to becoming a practitioner. "Why don't you take this to the next level? You know you can do it, and you can help even more people that way." He had only taken the first level of training at the Center and didn't feel compelled to go further. But during the past year, he could see a shift in her: Reiki was no longer a curiosity but was becoming a passion, and she was good at it. Besides, the weather was breaking, his golf clubs had just been freshly polished, and there were courses to play.

She took a long time to decide, but she always did that. She could make fast decisions about almost everything but herself.

When her business cards arrived and she saw her name on the scheduling software and the website, it finally was real. She stared at the biography on the website for a long time and wondered if others would think she was any good. Catharine had always told her students to show confidence and compassion in every session. Well, Olive thought, she definitely had the compassion down. *Now for the first part.*

Strangely, at about age eleven or twelve, she'd had a continuing fantasy that she was some kind of princess living on Earth who was really from another planet. Her superpower was that she could heal people just by touching them. When she learned about Reiki and started to have experiences that were almost like her childhood dreams, she was incredulous. It was almost as if she were living the dream. She didn't know then that the other part, the part about living on another planet, was also probably true.

The first few sessions were, thankfully, mostly with friends. As more appointments came in, she could tell she was more comfortable with the countless details of how to talk to a client, how to do a session, and how much to share when she got intuitive information. She realized that information seemed to be coming in more from her third eye than her hands. It all still amazed her at times, especially the intuitive part.

She was especially fascinated by the chakra system, the Eastern method of assessing wellness based on the flow of energy through the body. It made perfect sense to her that facing an emotional issue could impact every part of one's life and even affect the physical body. She could feel heaviness in someone's heart center long before she learned that a beloved pet had just died. She could tell that a client wasn't talking about something important when she felt as if her own throat were closing. It was like being a detective, trying to figure out the best way to help by understanding the emotional challenges each person was dealing with. It was even more rewarding when she could suggest something important that the client hadn't even considered.

She thought about how far she had come since her first Reiki session. Now she was no longer leery about guides and helpers; she depended on them, especially the ones who often appeared to help her in sessions. She also wasn't nervous about encountering a spirit attachment. In fact, she saw releasements as one of the most rewarding things she could do to help someone—not just her client but also the sad and lonely people who now found peace. She was still being challenged by new situations—actually, she hoped that would never stop. She followed the Center's mantra to always demonstrate confidence and compassion, and because of that, she was usually successful in helping her clients.

She was getting experience in determining if the appearance of a spirit in the session was perhaps from the client's previous life. If so, she was learning how to communicate with the soul to understand what was important about that lifetime, if there were missions or lessons, and if they had been learned. If the soul was then ready to move to the light, she would ask guides to please help.

She was just starting to find out about the shamanic concept of soul retrievals and the belief that pieces of human souls could splinter off during traumatic events. It was usually protective when a soul splintered—perhaps so that one didn't remember a horrific accident—but it was important to reunite all the missing parts when they were ready. She hadn't yet done her own soul retrieval but had watched her teachers perform some.

She was careful never to share a client's name or too many specifics about a session, but sometimes it took an hour and a glass of wine to share all of her adventures when she got home.

Much had changed since the first time she heard "It's time," especially in how she now connected to others and how many of her beliefs had changed. She wondered if maybe all the interesting things that happened to her, even the scary parts, were designed somehow to provide experiences or lessons. She wondered if there was a plan for everyone's life that just had to be discovered.

Jacob had been coming into the Center for several years before Olive met him. A professional man in his forties, Jacob was a regular client for pain relief for an achy knee. After he frowned at her once for sharing an intuitive message she received, she realized he didn't much care for woo-woo stuff, so that was quickly stopped.

During the seventh time she saw him, he relaxed enough to go into a deep sleep. She followed his breathing as it got deeper and more measured, followed by a couple of gentle coughs. His head slowly turned from side to side, and his lips moved as though they were trying to form words. Then the fingers of his right hand started to move, and the whole arm slowly rose into the air with the fingers waving and tapping out a message like Morse code. *Hmm*, she thought. *This doesn't look like sleep. And if this is a spirit attachment, it sure isn't acting like anything I've seen before.*

Then there were deep, almost guttural sounds. It appeared Jacob was trying to say something. He slowly arched his back, coming off the table about an inch, and several twitches all over his body followed. Then, with a light sigh, his entire body slowly settled back on the table.

"Jacob? Are you okay?" Olive asked.

"Hello, Olive Stuart" was the quiet response. After a long pause, he again spoke: "It's time."

Olive prided herself on handling just about everything that happened in a session, but she wasn't prepared for this. "Who are you?" she almost screamed. "You were the one talking to me before, weren't you?"

"Yes. Do not be afraid. I have come to talk to you. This is Avratar from the fifth dimension."

Fifth dimension? No one ever had told her she would be talking to aliens, not once in any class. She had mastered spirit attachments and past lives. She could almost do a soul retrieval, but this wasn't part of any curriculum so far, not even in internship. Now Jacob was gone, and a disembodied voice named Avratar was there instead.

Okay, maybe it really was a spirit attachment. It didn't feel like one, but she still checked just to make sure. Sometimes they could be pretty clever in the ways they tried to fool you. Sometimes they could look like someone she knew or an adorable puppy—anything to keep from being evicted. She knew they didn't want to go into the light at death, so they would do just about anything they could think of to maintain their safe status quo. She had heard stories that a basket of cobras could be projected right in front of you if you were afraid of snakes.

Since people's energies were all connected, she wondered if an earthbound spirit or maybe a real extraterrestrial had picked up on just how much she hated the whole idea of aliens. Talking to Artie about what had happened when she was young, including seeing aliens, wasn't the same thing as having one possibly on her table. She wondered if she was actually touching one or at least touching Jacob when he had one inside him.

Olive briefly considered more logical possibilities. She wondered if there were people who had alter egos come out during a session, as if she were working on Clark Kent, and instead, Superman started talking. She thought maybe Jacob was playing some kind of prank, but she quickly dismissed that. He wasn't the kind of guy to do that. He didn't even seem to like to hear a joke.

She strained to hear if another practitioner was walking in the hallway. Maybe someone else with more experience would know what was happening and what to do next.

When she finally found her voice, she heard it almost squeak with fear. "Why are you here? Why do you keep telling me that it's time?"

The voice was quiet and calm, with every word carefully spoken. "You have been selected from a mass of people to bridge the gap between humans and extraterrestrials. It is your responsibility to educate and improve the lives of those around you today and always, for you have been selected."

Was this some kind of perverse joke? She didn't want anything to do with extraterrestrials. She didn't want to see movies about them, she didn't want to read anything about them, and she sure as heck wasn't going to be any kind of bridge to them.

"Your role is to assist with the awareness of channeling love and understanding. Do not be afraid of what is to come." Jacob's right hand started moving again, with his fingers seemingly tapping a message. "There is limited time, and your help is needed."

"Sorry, Mr. Avratar, or whoever you are, but you'd better find somebody else."

She first assumed Jacob would want to know about someone talking through him, but the look on his face said otherwise. She had a feeling he might not schedule with her anymore.

When she got home, she assumed Artie would find it just as ridiculous as she had, but she was wrong. "What do you mean you're not going to do it?" Artie sounded angry. "They come from like a gazillion miles away to find you, and you aren't going to help?"

"You aren't really serious, are you? You don't really believe that this is all real, do you? Well, do you?" Olive could get just as angry, even though she had never before shown Artie that side of her. "I don't know which one of you is crazier—you or the guy I worked on today."

Their first fight was over extraterrestrials. She couldn't believe it. That made Olive even angrier. "What do you think I was supposed to do? Just tell him, 'Sure, I'll be glad to help'? Do I need to go to Venus or just the moon?"

"Look, all I'm saying is that you didn't even want to find out what it was all about. And I just don't get it. What if they picked you for something really important, and you're like, 'Nope, I'd rather go shopping'?"

That was a particularly low blow since Artie had been worried about their finances. She had thought she and Artie would have a good laugh over this and then talk about that day's golf game. Now their first fight was over extraterrestrials.

"Just stop it!" she screamed at him. "You know how I feel about all that stuff. What makes you think I'd even consider helping them? Even if it was real?"

Now each of them was hugging the far side of the mattress.

Even Jacob had been a little angry at her when she asked him how he was doing with everything that had happened. Not only did he not remember anything except enjoying a relaxing nap, but he had little patience for such nonsense about another voice coming out of him. Rubbish!

She didn't know what to do. What if it was all real, and they really did need her help? Why her? Would she have to actually look at an alien? What if they took her and put orange triangles on her again?

Chloe's reaction the next morning was just as surprising. "Wow, Olive, that's totally cool!" she exclaimed. "I mean, I remember all the stuff that happened a while ago, but what if those guys were the bad ETs, and now the good ETs want to work with you? How cool is that?"

Olive didn't even want to think about good ETs versus bad ETs. She just wanted all of them to go away.

"If you don't want to work with that ET guy, is it okay if I do?" Chloe was serious. "I mean, only if you're sure you don't want to work with him."

Olive just stared at her in disbelief.

Even if she decided to change her mind, she was pretty sure she would never hear from him again. Jacob could find plenty of practitioners who didn't do crazy talk. Maybe that Avratar dude had been just passing by Earth like a cosmic hitchhiker and stopped to take a break. All she knew was that others didn't seem to understand why she wasn't jumping up and down at the prospect of working with a galactic snake-oil salesman. Eventually, she let the experience fade from her memory.

A few weeks later, she was getting out of the shower, and she heard a light *click-click-click-click* coming from her phone. She stared in disbelief as a message was typed out by an invisible hand. Something was appearing letter by letter in front of her, as though she herself were typing: "Soon arrive. Please help." She realized that if she changed her mind about connecting with them, they were close enough to find her; maybe they would be angry if she said no again.

What happens if an alien gets angry? She didn't want to know. They were probably reading her mind right now. That meant they probably had been watching her in the shower. *Oh God, please, not again.*

Chapter 13

Is All This Real?

....

"Do you have a minute?" Olive asked the director. "I'm not sure how to deal with something."

"Sure," she replied. "I'm actually free for a while. What's up?"

Catharine listened intently as Olive spoke. Sometimes her voice was so quiet that Catharine had to lean in closely and strain to hear. Olive had only been on staff for about five months and had said more than once that she didn't want to do anything that might raise a red flag or cause problems. Management had often wondered where that continuing concern came from. Now she was obviously anxious or perhaps even frightened by something, so Catharine was pleased Olive trusted her enough to share something that was apparently so painful.

Olive's words were rambling and got more emotional by the minute. "I've never had anything like this happen before. I mean, I know you talked to all of us when we were students about possible contact with an ET, maybe in a session or in meditation. I don't know if you're okay with actually having an ET in the building or if all that talk about future contact was just theoretical. This is just all too weird, just saying this out loud." She was struggling to find the right words. "I had contact with an alien!" Olive blurted out.

"Wow. Okay," Catharine responded. "How? When?"

Olive's anxiety was palpable as she shared what had happened with Jacob a few weeks earlier.

"I certainly understand why that would have surprised you, but it feels like there's more to the story. Tell me why this experience with Jacob has frightened you so much."

Olive took a couple of deep breaths and then told her about all the frightening events in her life, including the stories from a few years ago and her terrifying experiences many years earlier. "I really thought all of this alien stuff was over with. Now this ET guy says he wants me to work with him. You don't understand. Just seeing a cartoon of a creature in a magazine kept me awake all night years ago, and once, I even fainted when I saw something on TV that reminded me of what I saw years ago. And now look at this," she said, showing the screenshot message that had been tapped out yesterday. "He's following me. I can't even hide! I thought it was over with. I just don't know anymore what is happening to me," Olive said quietly in desperation. "Is all this real?" Artie and Chloe seemed to think it was real; in fact, they couldn't believe she didn't jump at the chance to help the alien guy. She didn't know what to do.

When really young, Olive had loved to watch *Star Trek*; she and her brothers all had had plastic lightsabers from *Stars Wars*; and sometimes she'd gotten to stay up late to see a program on PBS about the Hubble telescope or what the rings of Saturn might look like. But when she saw old black-and-white movies from the 1950s about aliens coming to Earth, it was obvious they were people in plastic costumes. "I wasn't scared at all back then, when I was a little kid. In fact, I suppose I was like everyone else in wondering what life was like on other planets."

She had heard about the UFO crash in Roswell, New Mexico, and seen some *Project Blue Book* episodes on the History Channel. She even had followed some of the recent reports out of the Pentagon that the government was studying the whole ET and UFO thing, so even the military agreed it was all real. She wasn't sure if that was comforting or made her more afraid. "Look, I can go to Starseed and listen to everyone's stories. But I didn't think I would ever have any personal experience ever again. But here I am. Don't they know that I really don't want to have anything to do with them ever again?"

Olive wasn't sure why she was so upset. Was it because of things that had happened or of things that might happen? "Are there good ETs and bad ETs? What if the guy inside Jacob was a bad ET? Was it because I've been going to Starseed meetings and it's tracking me? And what about all those movies where they get inside your body and turn you into a zombie or machine? Do they want to come to eat us? Or make us their sex slaves?"

Catharine held her hand and tried to defuse the growing anxiety, as Olive was becoming more worked up with each terrifying scenario she imagined. "Whoa. How about if I jump in for a minute? I know how confusing it can be the first time you encounter something that completely throws you out of your comfort zone. Trust me, I've been there. I used to be just as afraid as you. Think back. Were you afraid while you were talking to—what was his name? Avratar?"

Olive said she hadn't been, not till later, when she'd had some time to think about it.

"So while you were talking to him, you were connecting out of your heart center, right? And that connection felt positive?" Catharine asked, and Olive nodded. "You're pretty intuitive. If something didn't feel right, I bet you would know right away."

Olive still wasn't as intuitive as she wanted to be, but she supposed that was somewhat accurate.

"We have quite a few people who are receiving messages right now from off-world beings. Some of the messages are through dreams or intuitive thoughts or even direct contact. Many of the messages are identical: that visitors would be arriving soon and that the purpose of their arrival is to help humanity and planet Earth." She asked Olive if she had ever heard of channeling.

Olive shook her head. That wasn't completely true, because it was one of the bad things her mother had warned her never to do.

"Actually, I think the United States is one of the few industrialized nations in the entire world that hasn't yet released our UFO files," Catharine said. "Most other countries are openly talking about all this. Makes you wonder what our leaders are so afraid of, doesn't it? My bet is they don't want us to know how much we've been lied to."

If it was true that beings from other planets actually existed, Olive couldn't understand why they would be coming in to help. "What could they possibly help with? And why would they even care or know what was happening on Earth? Don't they live on the other side of the universe?"

"Hmm. I'm afraid that's a topic that might be a lot larger than we have time for right now, but let me try to fill in a few blanks for you," Catharine said. "First of all, it's not that they are just now in contact with Earth. They've been here for thousands of years. Many, many thousands of years. In fact, some people think they were here long before humans. There are countless images of beings who don't look human all over the world—in caves, on rock art, in Egyptian tombs, in statues. Have you ever heard of the feathered serpent who created civilizations all through Central and South America? How about images of the Ant People in the American Southwest?"

Olive had but had figured those were just made-up pictures.

"Do you have any idea how hard it must have been for primitive people to carve images into rock? They wouldn't have done it if it hadn't been important to them."

Olive agreed that was probably so.

"So let's assume they've always been here and often interacted with humans, maybe even helping out when asked to. Like when the ancient Greeks or Romans asked their gods for help with a conflict or drought. Cultures all over the world have myths about how the gods created their civilizations, and there are countless tales about how these gods often traveled in flying chariots. Sounds like flying saucers to me.

"So this is how I understand it. Yes, they've always been here on Earth or at least checking in on us. Some people even believe they helped to create humanity, so they see us kind of like distant relatives. But they didn't want to interfere or influence people on Earth. Maybe this is one of the reasons why Earth is called a 'free-will planet.' Anyway, everything changed at the end of World War II, when we dropped two atomic bombs on Japan. I know you can't see them, but not all beings live in a 3D world. And not all beings live here on Earth. Some even live in higher dimensions."

Olive recalled that Avratar had said he was from the fifth.

"So dropping the atomic bombs was like a galactic SOS to the universe, sending out a huge mayday signal. A lot happened after that, including some far-reaching consequences. There was not only the potential of destroying the way of life for inter- or multidimensional beings but also the very real possibility of someday blowing up our entire planet. And if that happens, then we've altered the revolution of all planets around the sun. And who knows what would happen if all of those dominoes started to fall? We aren't talking about impacting people just here on Earth."

Olive was thoughtful. "And what happens to the balance with other solar systems?" She wasn't really expecting an answer, so the question hung in the air for a while. "The threat is real, isn't it? So many angry people have access to nuclear weapons right now."

"Let me mention something else, and then I'll have to get to my appointment. Look at how we have polluted the lakes and rivers, how the oceans are filled with plastic, and how smog is so intense in many cities that people have to wear masks. We're killing the bees with all the pesticides, the glaciers are melting, and there's so much warfare and genocide around the world." Her voice trailed off.

"They're really coming in to help, aren't they?"

Catharine understood how difficult it was for Olive to comprehend the enormity of that concept. "Yes, Olive, I really do believe they are coming in to help."

Chapter 14

Gaia Is Hurting

....

Olive usually worked at the Center in the evenings, taking appointments after she finished her full-time job. It made for long days, but she didn't get tired much. She assumed that was why it was called energy work. Plus, she had always heard that it wasn't work if one really enjoyed it.

Having an evening home with Artie seemed like a real treat—dinner, dessert, and just relaxing in the living room. She had picked up a book from the library on Atlantis that she was eager to look through. She wasn't sure why she was curious about the mysterious missing island, but it had come up in some conversation. Background chatter confirmed a commercial break for the hockey game, so she figured it was safe to share Plato's description of the continent in 360 BCE. Whenever she told Artie interesting facts, she was never sure if he really wanted to hear her or was just being polite. They both knew any conversation during overtime for the hockey game was off-limits.

She looked over at him in the recliner and saw his eyes closed and his mouth slightly open. A small snore sounded every few seconds. She wondered if this was what Mr. Excitement was like every evening around there.

She had always told him she loved the little squeak as he snored, but she never had her phone close enough to record him. She moved quietly toward the recliner and hit the voice recorder on her phone. *Got it!* In addition, there was a little clicking noise she hadn't heard before. She continued to record for a little bit and realized the little squeak was now gone, and the recording was all clicking noises, some of them a little louder than before. *Hmm.* She wondered what that clicking noise was. *Maybe a dream?*

Then there was a deeper intake of breath, and Artie's head gently moved from side to side, with his mouth moving as though it were trying to form words. He had a slight arch to his back. "Hello, Olive Stuart."

"Hello, Avratar."

"Thank you for allowing me to talk with you this evening."

She wasn't sure if she had a choice. "I didn't know if you would come back. I mean, I thought I might have hurt your feelings or something." Did aliens have feelings?

"There is much to talk about," he said, and she quickly looked at the voice recorder and hoped she was getting this all on tape. "You have questions."

"Yes, I suppose I do. I don't know who you are or why you picked me."

"I am Avratar from the fifth dimension."

"Right. I mean, why are you here? Not here in my living room but here on Earth."

"We are here to help. Your planet is hurting. Your people are hurting. Gaia is hurting."

"Who is Gaia?"

"Humans call her Mother Earth. She is hurting, and we have been called to help."

"Mother Earth called you? How?"

"She is a living being, as you are. You and she are as one. She and the universe are as one. Therefore, you and the universe are as one. When humans hurt, she hurts. And when she hurts, we all hurt. We will arrive soon to help humans. Time is limited."

"Who is *we*? More than you?"

"Yes, there will be many. We will come to help. You will also be contacted by others who are also here to help."

"Will I have to see you? I mean, talking is one thing …" Olive was already starting to get nervous about seeing something scary.

"You have much fear. I will help you to release this. Please give me your hands."

She wasn't sure what to do, so she leaned over to touch Artie's hands. After a couple of seconds, a light electrical charge seemed to start at his hands and race through her body. She made a slight noise of surprise.

"Now you will know that I am here as your friend."

He was right; she wasn't as afraid of him. *How did he do that?*

"I will leave now."

"Wait a minute! What do you want me to do? What do you mean there isn't much time?"

"We will meet again. Good night, Olive Stuart."

"Good night, Avratar." She added, "Thank you," even though she didn't really know what she was thanking him for.

The clicking started up again and then faded away. She saw twitching all over Artie's body, probably as Avratar was leaving, which woke Artie up. "What?" he said, looking up into her wide-eyed face. "Did I fall asleep?"

"You remember that guy who came through the client a few weeks ago? Avratar? Well, he was here tonight. Just now. Listen!"

A few minutes later, Artie said, "Well, that's definitely my voice, but I don't remember any of that." The recording was only about four minutes long, so they listened to it two more times. "How do you suppose they're going to help? Do they have technology to clean up the oceans? Are they going to fix climate change? I wonder who is coming. And why you?" He had all the same questions she did.

"Beats me." She was just glad she'd gotten something recorded so she could prove that it really had happened. The group of like-minded people she connected to these days would have believed her even without the recording, but it was nice to have proof. The other people, the ones who weren't really in her tribe any longer, wouldn't have believed her anyway.

"What do you suppose the clicking noise is?" she asked. "Do you think it's language? Maybe that's how he really talks." They looked at each other and shrugged. "I think I'm okay with working with him," Olive said.

The following week, she brought the audio recorder to a Starseed meeting. No one else at the meeting had ever gotten an alien talking on tape. Seeing several envious looks, she felt a little better about having been contacted. At least she wasn't nearly as scared. Maybe he had done something to her when he touched her. She wondered if everybody was afraid of something. Probably. She had a quick flash of being eleven years old again, a princess on a faraway planet who could help people with just a touch. Sometimes she wished she was eleven again.

"Have you heard from him lately?" one of the Starseed members asked.

She hadn't, she said, almost with a sigh. She didn't know how to call an alien. "Is there some kind of sign you put in a window or special whistle?" If they ever connected again, she would be sure to ask. She was actually hoping to hear from him again. She wasn't sure if Jacob had come back to the Center—at least he hadn't booked with her—and lately, the only noise out of Artie when he slept was that little squeak.

Chapter 15

Other Lives

....

"I think I need to learn to meditate better," Olive told Chloe one day. "I always thought I was doing it the right way, but maybe not. I start out okay, like I think I'm supposed to, but then my mind just goes off here and there, and pretty soon I'm writing memos in my head and doing shopping lists. How does somebody get to the nirvana stage?"

"I wouldn't know. Not my thing."

Sometimes it was just the two of them at lunch, and sometimes a few other staff joined them. Everyone had a different work schedule, which often happened when running community programs every day all day. But it was nice to see some of the people who mostly worked other shifts.

She didn't talk about energy work, spirituality, or any of her new interests much during her daytime job. At least not to anyone besides Chloe. She was pretty sure it would have been frowned on by her boss, and she didn't want everyone else to see how much she preferred being at the Center to being there. But her day job paid the bills. At least for now.

The other reason she didn't talk about it much was that she worked with people who didn't approve. Not that they did anything obvious to hurt her feelings, but they also didn't hide the fact that they thought she was doing something that was somehow anti-God. She understood; in fact, not long ago, she had thought the same, but it still made her sad. There were those who didn't want to hear anything that might conflict with something they already believed to be true. *We see what we want to see. We believe what we want to believe. We know what we want to know.*

That night, Artie was already asleep when she got home. She found a note on the dining room table, signed with a big heart, along with some cheese and a glass of wine. He really was a swell guy. She gathered everything and flopped down onto the couch to unwind. These evening hours were really messing with their time together, but both of them knew this was what Olive felt she should be doing. It also made the time they had together even more enjoyable.

She usually tried to meditate early in the morning, but that hadn't been very successful. She had too many mental lists to create or could hear the morning news shows on in the background. She wondered if evenings would be better, with less competition for her time and energies. She took another sip of the cabernet and closed her eyes.

After a few minutes, she saw a door forming in front of her, and she wondered why. Maybe she was supposed to go through it. She could tell she was relaxed, but she wasn't sure if it was the wine or just tiredness from the day. Either way, it felt nice. The door took the form of something she once had seen in a photo of an English country cottage. Actually, it didn't feel as if it were from a photograph; it seemed as though she really had seen the door once. But she had never been to England.

She saw herself walking up to the door and watched as a man's hand reached out to open it. *A man's hand?* That almost made her snap out of the meditation. He walked inside and took off his coat. This was his house, but it also felt like her house too. She saw him in the chair, but then she also could look around the room. She wondered why things looked familiar: people in a portrait over the fireplace and a vase on the table. She knew the layout of the house, including the back door that led to the garden, which was completely overgrown.

After a few minutes, Olive heard a clatter of nails on the wood floor. Max and Sophie realized she was home and wanted to play. She reluctantly left the dream, or whatever it was, and threw toys until they settled down again.

There was something recognizable about that house and even that man. She made a mental note to schedule a past-life regression to see what might come up. It would be wild to see a previous life. Was she him?

Maybe she was a daughter or something. Maybe she'd also schedule an Akashic records session to see how her current life might connect with all her other lives.

She thought about settling into the visualization again but instead heard a loud crack overhead. By now, she realized this was usually associated with the arrival of a guide or helper. She threw out a quick protection just in case and a request that only beings from the highest light be permitted in that space; all others were forbidden to enter the protected space or impact her in any way.

She was actively trying to build her intuitive skills and could already see huge shifts. The psychic development classes helped her to discern which messages were for her highest good and which should be discarded. Before, she hadn't even known she had a choice. As she became more and more sensitive and aware of the signals around her, she knew it was even more important to stay in a safe place.

Her left side became cold and tingly, and she supposed a guide was nearby. She was glad she no longer resisted connecting with invisible helpers, especially since they were consistently incredibly supportive, not just during sessions but also in helping her with all the big and small details of life. But something about this was different, starting with an odd pinging sensation at the top of her head, right at the crown. This energy was different; there was an intensity she hadn't felt before. She knew she was well protected, so she was mostly curious, not concerned. This definitely was not her mother since there was no stinky perfume. Then she heard the words inside her head: "Hello, Olive Stuart."

It was just like when she'd heard the voice on New Year's Day in her head many years ago. It even sounded the same. "Avratar, is that you?"

"Yes, there is much to discuss and much that you will need to share with others. I would like you to learn how to channel. Is this agreeable?"

She nodded and then wondered if he could tell she nodded.

"We will start with my energy. How does it feel to you?"

"Strong—really strong. But friendly. And safe."

"This is good. Now please listen as I communicate an important phrase to you: *Om la shanti de la ta.* Om la shanti de la ta. Om la shanti de la ta."

Wow, she thought. She was really hearing it inside her head, just like the first times he had talked to her. Was this channeling? She had thought it would be a lot harder. She repeated the phrase over and over as the session ended, and then she headed upstairs to bed and lay next to that beautiful, soft squeak.

The next morning, Artie asked her, "Did you have a rough night, babe?" He was already reaching for a coffee cup for her.

"I don't think so. Why?"

"I thought maybe it was a bad dream or something. You kept saying, 'Om something something something,' over and over."

She accepted the coffee. "Om la shanti de la ta. It means 'Spirit of sound and light.' Avratar taught it to me last night while I was channeling." She grinned at him and took a sip.

Part 2

Awakening

Chapter 16

Quieting the Mind

....

It was getting harder and harder to be at her daytime job, when all Olive wanted to do was healing work full-time. She and Artie had talked about it several times, but their budget just didn't allow it. Juggling two jobs had its frustrations, especially when a work meeting ran over and she arrived late for a 6:00 p.m. appointment. Bad weather, or good weather but bad traffic, was even more infuriating. Some days, she said Avratar's om chant over and over for the half-hour commute just to calm down. It was a bad idea to show up stressed out for a relaxation appointment.

She never missed Starseed Connections, but she was also becoming a regular at a number of other groups, such as an empath support group. There was no doubt about it: she was waking up to new ideas and, even more importantly, discovering how she fit into this emerging reality. She had heard the younger clients once say that she was woke. She just knew she had an insatiable appetite for all of this, and the more she learned, the more she wanted to know.

Sometimes she felt she wasn't actually learning new things but was remembering. She wasn't sure why that was, but things she shouldn't have known anything about sounded familiar. She wondered if it was a past-life thing, or perhaps she was tapping into the universal consciousness, which was often called the Akasha. She was especially drawn to interesting healing techniques, such as tapping, which activated acupressure points on the body to change belief systems or enhance affirmations. She often thought, *If our subconscious holds that kind of power, what else can it do?*

She was connecting with Avratar more often now and felt his energy even if they didn't talk. It was somehow reassuring that it seemed he was checking on her every so often. At first, she was worried that it was mostly her imagination and that she wasn't really hearing him. She supposed everyone thought that when he or she first started to get messages. When she told someone in Starseed that she thought Avratar was nearby, he said he agreed; he sensed him too. That was when she realized others also connected with him. Then there was the time someone shared information he had received from Avratar the night before, and Olive was surprised she had received the same message. *Maybe we all hear from him.* She wondered how all of that worked.

Many of the other Starseed members were also now in regular communication with other nonhumans. Sometimes the star beings introduced themselves and said where they were from, but no one knew enough about faraway star systems to completely understand. Sometimes they said they were from a specific dimension. That was even more baffling. Members wondered what the difference was between the different dimensions and how many dimensions there were. Also, how was it possible that ETs and interdimensionals could both communicate with Earth people? They would have to ask Avratar.

One night's discussion focused on what they should call their new contacts. Someone made a joke that maybe they were really the guides and helpers people asked for help. After a quick chuckle, everyone fell silent, as that possibility was suddenly real. What if that were true? Everyone agreed the information and contacts felt positive. That was especially important since everyone had been fooled by tricksters, earthbound spirits who wanted them to believe they were really in contact with a divine being instead of someone who had felt too unworthy to go into the light at death. Some suggested calling them off-world beings. Olive made a mental note to ask Avratar if that term was okay with him.

Some people were reluctant to say they could channel, acknowledging that the term *channeling* could be emotionally charged for some of their families and friends, so they just said they got messages. No one was positive which contacts lived in other dimensions and which came from another planet. If one was an inter- or multidimensional being, did that mean it didn't come from a planet? Or did it live on a ship? Were there cities in these other dimensions? Was the fifth dimension just like the third dimension but maybe vibrating at a different level? Olive thought maybe it was like turning the radio dial a little bit to get a whole new signal. She had heard that it was okay to call them persons but not okay to call them aliens. It was all interesting. She just hoped she didn't do something to offend an entire species.

There were eight Starseed members who showed up the night that someone suggested a group meditation. "Should we ask for someone specific or just be open to anybody? How long should we try?" Someone asked if a half hour was long enough or maybe too long. A gentle chime from someone's phone was set for thirty minutes, and the lights were turned down.

The term *meditating* was still a little intimidating to Olive. At first, she had been afraid she was supposed to twist herself into pretzel poses to do it right, but then she'd learned that it was mostly just quieting one's mind. Sometimes she could relax just by listening to soft music, and she often felt she was also in that relaxed space when she was driving long distances, and her mind was on autopilot. Somebody once had said, "When you pray, you talk to God; when you meditate, God talks to you." That seemed about right. She still didn't feel she was good at it, but she was better than she had been a few months ago. Thank goodness there wasn't a quiz.

With palms upward on her lap, she first imagined there was a single candle flame in front of her, and she tried to shoo everything else from her mind. Every so often, a rogue image or reminder of something she had to do would creep into her awareness; after acknowledging it, she saw it recede back into the shadows. She discovered that trying to ignore the invading thoughts didn't work well for her. They never really seemed to go away; they just lurked in the background.

Someone shifting in a chair, a sniffle, and other background noises melted away. She could feel her body releasing any tightness from the day's hassles, followed by anything that took up too much energy in her mind. There was a softness that seemed to envelop her now. She let the softness surround her.

After a few moments, she clearly heard the familiar "Hello, Olive Stuart." After she silently returned the greeting, Avratar stated that tonight she would learn how to further open her third eye, the center of intuitive insight and vision. This would be an important step toward increasing communication with those who were already there and those who would soon arrive. Olive hadn't considered there might be others already present. She wondered if they were also communicating with people all over the planet, or perhaps they had different jobs. She thought maybe he was nicely telling her she was meditating the wrong way. Then, as if in answer to her unspoken question, he added, "Yes, you have started to open your vision, but there is much more to do. Let us begin."

He suggested that holding a clear quartz crystal would help to increase the vibration. She wondered if there was one in her pocket. No. Nearby? She couldn't tell with her eyes closed and the lights down. Her wedding ring! It wasn't a huge diamond, but she supposed it would work.

"Now rotate the crystal in a circular pattern counterclockwise around your third eye several times. Remove any energetic debris from your brow, and see it being carried by the breeze. Now see colors begin to form, perhaps only a few at first and then more. Watch as the colors move around you."

She figured if circling her wedding ring a few times would be good, doing it for a few minutes longer must be better. She hoped she hadn't scraped a circle into her brow. At some point, she felt she was ready for the next step and used her other hand to brush away anything that had been cleared from her sixth chakra. She even made a motion to scoop out anything remaining and held it up to be blown away. As she did, she saw a small pastel-pink orb dancing in front of her, then a light green bubble, and then a little baby-blue circle. They all began to move slowly toward the left, and as they did, more bubbles came into her field of vision from the right. Then more and more came, rotating faster and faster. Now they were moving so quickly that the colors became blurs. She became dizzy and was briefly concerned she might fall out of her chair. Was this the same experience others were having? She hoped so, because so far, this was amazing.

Then it all changed. The colors slowed down and stopped rotating. She watched as they transformed into millions of twinkling stars all around her. She was somehow gliding through the cosmos, which had become shades of lavender, pinkish lilac, and deep purple. She had heard people talk about seeing violet while in a deep meditation; this must have been what they were talking about. Whatever was happening, she felt more peaceful than she had ever felt. She was pretty sure she didn't have a body anymore—at least she couldn't see her hands and feet. It was as though she were pure energy.

She wondered if she was floating for only a few minutes or eternity; she didn't know, and she didn't care. It seemed she was receiving information, or at least she knew the information was accessible, but she didn't want to lose this feeling even to think about it or go retrieve anything. She had somehow merged with a vast consciousness, an awareness. This must have been what Avratar was talking about when he said that she was part of Earth and that Earth was part of the universe, so she was part of the universe. That was what it felt like. She felt as if she were a drop of water in the ocean. Or maybe an ocean in a drop of water. She felt embraced and surrounded by it. The universe was in her, and she was in it. Maybe this was what God was.

"Olive?"

Was this real? If it wasn't, she didn't want the hallucination to stop. All she had to do was think about something, and she knew she could connect to it. She was part of all the stars, all the planets, and everything in between. The violet was pulsing with life, as though it were filled with everything that ever had been and everything that ever would be.

"Olive!"

She was being moved gently back and forth.

"Olive, come back."

No! No! It was all going away—the beautiful violet, the information, the love, and the awareness. *Please don't bring me back!* They weren't prepared for her explosive anger when she opened her eyes. "Why did you do that?" she yelled at the circle who had gathered around her. "Why did you bring me back?"

Their worried faces looked stunned, and she immediately apologized. She attempted to explain what she had experienced, from Avratar's instructions to use clear quartz to the flying colors to floating in the nothingness and the everythingness. She couldn't really objectively communicate what had happened, because she still wasn't beyond that experience; she still had part of the feeling in her. She wasn't still floating in the purple, but she was still connected. It was as though the purple were still inside her. It had something to do with finally allowing herself to be supported by something she didn't understand but knew to be true. In every cell and every ounce of consciousness, she knew she was held and loved. Maybe that was the definition of faith.

She realized she had allowed herself to move to another level of awareness. She even felt different. It had something to do with trust, but she would have to give this more thought. She had thought about trust a lot in the past few years. Could she trust her parents to keep her safe, even in the scary times? Could she trust Artie to always be around to protect her? Could she trust others not to ridicule her if they didn't understand? Now could she trust the universe, whatever that was, to help her get to a higher level of awareness? She remembered seeing YouTube videos of firemen desperately trying to save puppies drowning in storm sewers while the terrified puppies were biting them. She really hoped she wasn't like a terrified puppy who ran away when helpers arrived.

Everyone made a mental note to find some clear quartz.

Chapter 17

Different Beings

....

Olive still saw off-world beings regularly, mostly in her mind's eye just as she was waking up. Every morning, there was a species she hadn't seen before, as though a different race had won the lottery for that day. They often continued in her consciousness for a moment or two after she opened her eyes, giving her a little extra time to get used to seeing them and remember details. She wondered if that was the purpose since Avratar had said she was supposed to be working with them someday. Maybe they were introducing themselves to her: "Howdy, strange-looking human!"

One morning, she got the distinct impression she was being studied. It wasn't just that someone was in front of her; he was looking at her as a biologist might look at a newly discovered form of life. She hadn't before thought about off-world beings having a consciousness or a specific purpose for their expedition to Earth. She felt a little like a specimen under a microscope or something in a zoo. She wondered if that was how tribes in the remote Amazon reacted to the presence of sociologists who came to study them.

When the images of different beings first started to flash in her mind every morning, her first thought was that they had come to hurt her, just like the ones who had come into her bedroom. But one day she started to question if the first ones, the ones in her bedroom, had really tried to hurt her. Other than the orange triangles, they really hadn't done anything to her. If she checked with her heart, she thought that every one of the beings she saw seemed to be friendly. She realized that her first thought that they were scary possibly had been because they were unfamiliar. *Maybe we always are afraid of the things we don't know anything about.*

She was still seeing them almost every morning, and even after all this time, they didn't do anything but look at her. They hadn't given the impression they were trying to hurt her. Looking back on that first scary night, she now wondered if maybe they had been just trying to say hello. Did they know they had frightened her? She occasionally thought about what first contact between Earth's astronauts and residents in another star cluster might look like. *What if we landed on another planet and wanted to meet its occupants?* Olive thought. *They would be just as terrified as I was.*

The orange triangles on her left arm were long gone now, but she still wondered about them. What if the beings were somehow tracking humans the way humans tracked whales, eagles, or bears? *If so, why would they want to track us? Why would they even care about us?* Then she started to wonder, *Why is it okay to put computerized chips in our dogs or in dolphins without asking them if they want one? How about putting a hot branding iron on cattle or a band on a bird's foot? If you think about it, every animal is probably terrified by the experience, even though we think we're somehow helping them. And how about all those birds covered by oil in an offshore rigging disaster?* Did they know the humans were trying to save their lives when the oil needed to be scrubbed off? *Maybe that's also what we humans often do: bite the person who is trying to help.*

There were many different perspectives.

The first time she saw a being staring at her in the morning, her heart raced for an hour. She knew it wasn't part of her dream of beautiful landscapes and a birthday party. All of a sudden, the party was replaced by somebody staring at her for a couple of seconds—someone with huge eyes and grayish-green skin who was maybe a foot away from her. That meant it was really in front of her and not part of the dream. After a week or so, she was no longer afraid to see them, although sometimes it could still be disconcerting.

Sometimes an appearance was accompanied by a word or a phrase. That had been happening more often lately. She believed she was most receptive to messages during that gauzy waking-up time, even more so than at 3:00 a.m., so it probably made sense to drop a message into her in the early hours. Once, the phrase was "Gratitude and forgiveness." She was struggling to get over a tiff with a coworker, so the timing seemed perfect.

She was a little embarrassed to admit that holding on to the anger would only hurt her, since she was pretty sure the coworker was so obstinate that she would never apologize. Once, she heard the word *judgment*. She wondered if that had to do with her comment about the pigheaded coworker. She wanted to assume it was a general suggestion but had to acknowledge that maybe she could be a little judgmental. She sighed when she wondered if she was more like her mother than she wanted to accept.

Then there were times when she woke up hearing music or even singing along to a familiar song. Once, she was singing along to Led Zeppelin's "Stairway to Heaven" as she awoke. After humming the song for hours one morning, she decided to check the lyrics on the computer to see if that would get the incessant tune out of her head. After she read the words and interpretations, she realized there was no way on Earth she could have put such a powerful message in her head.

Then there was the being she saw one morning and still remembered clearly even long after. It was snow white, soft and rounded, and not very tall, with soft, rolling arms and legs. She only saw her in profile—she had no idea why she thought it was female, unlike most of them—but the most striking feature was the most beautiful pair of soft dark eyes she had ever seen. They reminded Olive of a newborn fawn, trusting and gentle. A few days later, an intuitive at the Center asked her if she knew there was some kind of white being standing right next to her. When she described exactly what Olive had seen, it was confirmation that the beings she was seeing every morning weren't just projected images. They were really there.

Sometimes they looked human or so close they could easily have passed for one. Some of them were tall and thin, often with long blond or white hair. They were probably the ones called Nordics or Tall Whites, since they looked as if they could have come from Scandinavia. Then there were the ones that had facial features that kind of resembled a cat or a dog. Sometimes only the shape of the eyes were a little different. Sometimes the head was larger or even significantly longer than a human's. They were also different heights, anywhere from eighteen inches to maybe eight feet or higher. She had been told there were even some who were fifty feet tall. Judging by some of the massive prehistoric structures discovered all over the world, she could see that as a possibility. Some of them wore tunics or outfits of some kind, but most didn't have any clothes.

There were also ones often called Grays because of their grayish skin color, and she guessed those were the ones who had come into her bedroom. Around four feet tall, they usually had a small, flat nose; a small mouth; and large dark eyes, with a head that was usually much wider at the forehead than at the chin. Sometimes they looked almost childlike and sometimes like grumpy old men. She wondered if they aged, as humans did.

She occasionally saw one of the insectoid races but not as often. She had seen images of what they were supposed to look like and was pretty sure she would have remembered seeing one. She was especially intrigued by the group called the Mantids, ones who looked like praying mantises, because they were known to be the healers of the cosmos. She wondered how they did their healing and if they only worked on other Mantids.

She saw her first off-world being in the daytime while she was working on a young girl who was about nine years old. Her mother was seated nearby, staring intently at her phone, checking email or maybe playing card games. The girl had already been to several specialists who were unable to determine the source of stomach pain. Halfway through the session, Olive wondered if she might be able to ask for help from some of the beings who regularly visited her. She didn't think that would be a problem, but she wasn't sure about protocol. She wasn't even sure if there was a protocol manual somewhere. Maybe she was supposed to create one.

A few minutes later, a chill rolled into the room, and Olive automatically threw out another protection around all three of them just in case. Her jaw dropped open when, only a few feet away, a five-foot being she recognized as a Mantid appeared in shades of dark green with long antennae. Leaning slightly forward, using his long fingers, he touched the girl's stomach. The image only lasted for a second at the most, but her final view was of him slightly turning to face her before fading. The mom was still engrossed in solitaire and didn't realize how astounding the experience had been. But Olive knew, and she sent even more gratitude when the little girl said her pain was gone.

Olive wondered if it was possible to enlist their help for all other sessions. She wondered if an off-world being could be a guide. That seemed like an intriguing question. Perhaps they all worked together. Avratar had said that other humans would start to connect with the helpers at some point. She added that to the list of things that would dramatically shake up life on Earth if their visits became more public.

She was excited about the Mantid visit and especially excited that her little client's pain was gone, but she wasn't sure whom to tell or if she should even mention it at all. Artie still asked her about her day when she got home, and she couldn't wait to share this with him. Actually, there wasn't much she didn't share with him; fortunately, he never acted as if he didn't believe her. It seemed that everything happening to her was getting more and more dramatic these days. She was seeing more and knowing more, but there were many others also saying that. The practitioners were experiencing huge shifts in awareness, but so were many of the clients. Olive could share adventures with Starseed as long as she kept the client's name confidential; in fact, she realized that some members' experiences shared in meetings were even weirder than her own stories, and hers were pretty weird.

She was starting to discern which clients would be open to hearing intuitive information. What if there were people who were so afraid of extraterrestrials or hearing about guides being nearby that they would never come back to the Center? She was starting to realize that all of the rough experiences she'd had a few years ago had prepared her for where she was now. She was more compassionate when people talked about their anxieties. She knew that what seemed foolish and irrational to some people could be downright crippling to others.

Olive still wasn't sure how to help people get past their apprehension of extraterrestrials, especially with all the movies about invading aliens blowing up the White House. Maybe she was expected to use her own experiences to help people get beyond their fears. After all, not long ago, she had lived in a constant state of terror, and now she was welcoming a Mantid into the studio. Life was weird.

She still didn't have a lot of direct contact with the beings, but considering where she had been before she was woke and where she was now, she could almost understand how problems could start between different races or cultures on Earth. *If you have always thought that you were somehow better than others or that another group was somehow going to hurt you, you would also believe that those groups were somehow a threat or maybe that they shouldn't even exist.*

She once asked Avratar if all ETs were there to help, and if not, how would she know who were the good ETs and who were the ones who had their own agenda? He didn't give a direct answer but told her to trust her heart. He said, "If you trust, then we trust." She would rather have had everyone wear a white hat or a black hat to make her life much easier. She still wasn't sure how the white hats were going to help, but she didn't feel there was any reason not to believe them, especially Avratar. Maybe he was like the ambassador for the galactic Red Cross. If anything, the ones she saw each morning seemed to be especially sensitive that they might frighten people. If they had been there to take over the planet, she figured they would have done it by now.

She once asked Avratar what he looked like, and he replied that he would send her an image. Weeks later, she still didn't know and was embarrassed to admit she must not have been good at receiving. When one day she saw a dark figure walking in front of her in the studio during a treatment, she immediately protected her client and herself and then silently demanded to know who it was.

"Olive, it's Avratar," he replied softly.

She finally saw him: about six feet tall, with a large, oval-shaped dark head and long dark limbs. He looked just like one of the Ant People, who were revered around the world, especially by the Hopi Indians in the American Southwest. Olive wasn't sure it would ever be possible to hug Avratar, but she wanted to.

An intuitive student drew a sketch of Avratar about six months later. The student was nervous about telling Olive what she had seen in the room while they were working on someone, for fear she would be seen as some kind of kook. The student's confidence soared after Olive confirmed everything she had seen. The best part was that now Olive had a sketch of Avratar.

While she often saw images and heard songs in the early morning, she was also getting used to waking up around three o'clock in the morning, which was supposed to be the time when the veil between the worlds was thinner. She wasn't sure what that meant, but she felt she was more open to receiving messages around then. Sometimes it was exactly at 3:00 a.m., which always seemed interesting to her, as though someone purposely woke her up to say hi. Usually, it was Avratar, but she was starting to also hear from other beings. Some of them were helping her to become even more intuitive or helping to heal something in her body that didn't feel right.

One being said he was shifting something in her energy field to permit her to connect with higher vibrations. She wasn't sure what he was doing, but she trusted that it would somehow help. He asked if it was permissible to temporarily change the color of her dark brown eyes during the energy shift. They would be blue for a while, then green, and then return to brown. Olive was thrilled. Finally, she had something physical to confirm their contact! A few weeks later, a girlfriend remarked in bewilderment that her eyes were now blue. Soon after that, a coworker commented that she didn't remember her having green eyes. Olive ran to find a camera.

Occasionally, she woke up enough to reach for a small book light and her journal to record a dream or keep track of an intuitive message. She always used that time to give herself a quick treatment and check herself for anything that might need to be released. Usually, she was awake for only five or ten minutes before drifting off to sleep again. It was a fairly familiar ritual that confirmed she was becoming more intuitive.

When she woke up in the middle of the night a few weeks later, she could sense that someone was in the room. But as soon as she tried to get into a more comfortable position, she immediately knew this was different. Something was wrong. There was a low, metallic hum in the room that she had never heard before, but more importantly, she couldn't move, not one muscle. She was wide awake and could hear Artic's little squeak. She couldn't yell for help; she couldn't move a finger. There was something next to the bed.

If she could have taken a full breath, she might have hyperventilated from the fear. But she couldn't even take a deep breath. Whatever it was felt threatening. Was it going to kill her by not letting her breathe?

She was frightened. Why couldn't she move? She was certain that something was being done to her; it wasn't a stroke or anything like that. But what was it that was so near to her?

She hadn't felt this kind of panic for a long time. This wasn't like feeling Avratar's energy or sensing the beings who visited every morning. This was dark and menacing. This energy was ominous and sinister. She tried to send out a protection but was pretty sure it was too late. It was already there, and it wasn't leaving. She begged for help from God, Archangel Michael, and Avratar.

Every muscle in her body strained to fight against the attacker. She wanted to move her head to see what was doing this to her. Artie had said he would protect her, but she couldn't even make a gurgling noise to get him to wake up. This wasn't like being suffocated by the ghost when she was a kid. Whatever it was had paralyzed her entire body.

She had no idea how long she was struggling, but after what seemed like forever, one finger finally could move. That gave her hope that the rest of her body might also break free from its control.

Then it was over. She flailed in bed, moving every limb, until Artie woke up, and she tried to tell him how awful it had been. He kept saying it was just a nightmare, holding her until they both finally fell asleep.

But it wasn't a dream—and it wasn't a dream the next night or the one after that. Something was coming into the bedroom and paralyzing her. It happened three nights in a row, and once again, she felt targeted.

She researched night paralysis and night terrors and discovered that the phenomenon had been studied for hundreds of years. The medical community viewed it as a mental illness of sorts. There were hallucinations, sometimes from unresolved emotional issues or maybe poor diet. Suggestions to avoid recurrence included getting as much sleep as possible or perhaps not sleeping on one's back.

Olive wasn't hallucinating, and there was nothing wrong with her diet. There had been something in the room for the past three nights. It was evil, and it was controlling her body. All the medical websites agreed she should stop sleeping on her back.

That was the final straw for Olive. Western medicine could fix a broken arm but not a broken spirit. Allopathic medicine had failed her when she really needed answers as well as a good night's sleep. She needed to find someone who understood.

The being staring at her the next morning wasn't soft and white and certainly wasn't friendly looking. It was large and dark greenish-brown, with a dark expression Olive interpreted as threatening. She had never seen anything like it except in books. She was pretty sure it was a Reptilian, and she was pretty sure it was the being paralyzing her at night. She also had a feeling he was purposely staring at her to intimidate and frighten her. The old Olive would have crumpled like a used napkin; the new Olive was angry. Now she had to figure out what to do about it.

Chapter 18

Opening the Third Eye

....

Olive was becoming more intuitive, but sometimes she wasn't sure that was a good thing. She was pretty successful in protecting herself from others' emotions and drama, but she also was starting to have a greater awareness of things she sometimes wished she didn't know. When they went to dinner with Bill and Sue, she somehow saw them arguing in their living room and heard the word *divorce*. She seemed to know when something bad was going to happen, because her mood would turn dark. It was difficult for her to go into places where there was a lot of emotion, such as airports or hospitals, especially if she was a little tired or was dealing with her own stuff. Someone suggested she was an empath and encouraged her to find out how to see this gift as beneficial.

The best part about being more intuitive was that she seemed to be able to help her clients in ways she couldn't before. Her sessions had changed from excellent to off the charts. She was better at listening to messages from Spirit, like when she would hear a suggestion to mention something or to put her hands in a certain place to get even better results. Her schedule was mostly filled with referrals and returning clients. If only she could do this work full-time, she often thought.

The hardest part about being more intuitive was that she seemed to be more aware of things she had never before even thought about. Ever since she'd heard, "It's time," on New Year's Day many years ago, she'd told people she was living a charmed life. It was as though a whole new exciting world had opened up for her. Meditations were deeper and more insightful, and a wealth of information seemed to be more accessible. She was more peaceful, handling challenges with a calmness she never before had felt. She felt a deeper connection to guides, including all the beings she was working closely with. She was happier than she ever had thought possible.

But being more intuitive also meant she now saw things she hadn't seen before, including things that were uncomfortable, sad, and even frightening. If there was an on-off switch, it was definitely on. She wished she could have asked for it to be turned on just a little bit or turned on only to see happy things. In her first Reiki class, another student had said, "I really, really, really want to see my spirit guide, but don't show me anything scary." It didn't work that way.

Besides, she thought, *how is your guide going to know what scares you? Do you really know how you are going to react if Grandma suddenly appears right in front of you, when she transitioned years ago?*

Olive started to take classes to understand what it meant to be an empath and how to navigate some of the challenges that came with it. *Do you strengthen your protection or decide it's safer not to go to the mall? Do you watch the TV news, knowing how sad you might become at some of the images, or maybe just scan the headlines on your phone when you get a minute?* She could become physically ill when she saw instances of hurricane devastation or photos from a war zone. Sometimes the overwhelming sadness and inhumanity were too hard to handle.

She pretty much stopped going to the movies, because she couldn't handle feeling completely trapped in a theater with the volume way too loud and the images far too graphic. She also avoided the living room when Artie was watching police dramas, cable news shows fixated on the latest tragedy, or goofy game shows that featured ridiculous people who screamed continuously. When she had been a kid, hardly anyone had gotten shot, and now there were active-shooter drills in elementary schools and crazy people blowing up people in synagogues and day-care centers. She wondered when all of this had become the new normal and why others didn't hate this new normal as much as she did.

She discovered she wasn't alone; she met countless people like her at the Center. She had heard that one of Catharine's messengers, Gaia, had informed her that the Center was to serve as a meeting place, as the anchor, for those who wanted to connect with others. Catharine said she had nodded in agreement, but apparently, Gaia thought she hadn't fully understood her message. She patiently explained once again that what had been created was the center, with a small *c*, the hub of the wheel, the middle. Well, it definitely was that for people who were looking for a new path.

She discovered there were plenty of others who hated the violence of football games, so she was always busy with appointments during many sporting events. People who were moving into this newer awareness didn't follow hard rock as much as they used to and instead seemed to listen to R&B or light jazz. Some started to listen to radio stations that were more openly spiritual, with uplifting messages of hope and encouragement. Many people stopped drinking alcohol or eating meat. She saw a lot of familiar faces in the empath discussion group. It was a growing tribe.

She knew the shift affected people in different ways, but she was still a little angry that she couldn't enjoy a glass of wine at the end of the night or a beer with pizza anymore. Some people made the emotional decision to stop drinking, but for her, it was only physical. Lately, as soon as she drank anything, she would get sick, and hard stuff, such as bourbon, sometimes acted like pure caffeine. After one drink, she was wide awake all night. Why couldn't she get sick from eating broccoli?

There was also sadness when she talked to people who knew they were changing, while the people around them were not. Some no longer felt comfortable in talking to friends and family about their new interests, as others didn't understand, made fun of them, or even told them it was wrong to follow those beliefs. It wasn't uncommon for them to feel as if they didn't fit into their own families anymore. Relationships changed, and sometimes marriages ended. Even with all the challenges, Olive never heard someone say the new awareness wasn't worth it.

She was learning to navigate how increased intuition showed up in her daily life. Some of the discussions in her empath classes focused on what were sometimes called the *clairs*, which often included clairvoyance, or enhanced seeing; clairaudience, or enhanced hearing; clairsentience, or enhanced feeling; clairalience, or enhanced smelling; clairgustance, or enhanced tasting; and claircognizance, or enhanced knowing.

She wished she could see auras, as some people could, but then she realized that might be more of a distraction than she wanted to deal with. *Be careful what you wish for.* Then she wondered if people who saw auras felt sorry for those who couldn't.

Artie loved the way her new skills could help find his missing car keys or remind him of something important. He wasn't as happy, though, with her ruining a special surprise by guessing what they were going to do for her birthday.

Before becoming woke, she'd believed the New Age baloney that one should never even think about sad or dark things, because doing so would only attract more of them. She wondered why she ever had believed that, because darkness didn't care if one believed in it or not. Now she thought that knowing about something was the first step to protection. She worried about people who didn't see the need to protect themselves and didn't even want to hear about it. *Good grief,* she thought. *You know about burglars, so you put locks on your doors. You know that fire is a possibility, so you buy insurance. Why wouldn't you want to protect yourself from things that have an even greater likelihood of hurting you?*

Sometimes it felt as though a heaviness followed her home from the mall or the grocery. She would come home exhausted and cranky. She wasn't sure if the grouchiness was in her or in the home, so everything got cleared. She was much better about protecting herself at the Center, where protection and clearing afterward were part of the protocol. She just wished she would always remember to do it at other times. She suspected she probably had carried things home with her long before her third eye was blasted wide open, but before, she hadn't known about those things. She had stopped believing in the adage that ignorance was bliss a long time ago, especially when so much was at stake. But she couldn't deny that sometimes she missed being blissfully unaware. There were times when she was almost envious of people who said they weren't at all intuitive. They didn't know and probably didn't care that there was an invisible world that might be working against them. Unfortunately, when the ostrich's head was in the ground, the biggest target was in the air.

Olive especially enjoyed learning how to identify and release energy cords, spirit attachments, curses, and implants. They even discussed dark entities and demonics in case they ever encountered one. The instructor acknowledged that their chance of ever seeing truly dark entities was slim, but she wanted to make sure they at least had an awareness. It was fascinating to Olive that there were so many esoteric ways in which one's emotional and physical health could be impacted by negative energy and beings. She wondered why this information was so well known all over the world but rejected by Western medicine. What a shame to think that option to help wasn't offered.

She also wondered why so many energy workers didn't incorporate these advanced clearing techniques into their practices. She figured maybe they were never taught, or perhaps they just didn't want to think about it. Either way, it didn't make sense to her, especially since one couldn't possibly help his or her clients if he or she didn't know about all the options, including the scary ones. Maybe that was why she'd gotten the word *judgment* a while ago as she was waking up.

She had to learn quickly about psychic attacks when a new client astrally projected into her car on the way home. When she greeted him before their session, she thought she saw a cockiness or arrogance, perhaps a little condescension. During the session, she had the distinct impression his consciousness had left his body, as she suddenly couldn't feel his energy field, but she wasn't sure why or where it had gone. She knew it wasn't uncommon for a client to be temporarily out of body when there were particularly painful issues starting to come up. Olive suspected people all did that. But this time, she was certain he knew exactly what he was doing, because she intuitively saw him lying on the floor, looking up her skirt. "Get back in your body now!" she yelled. The man on the table formed a slight smile and a little chuckle before he eventually complied. After the session, Olive made it clear he would never do that again; his only response was the same little smile.

As she was driving home, Olive thought about the man who had chuckled earlier in the evening, wondering if there was anything she could have done differently. This was a first for her, and she tried to recall what she had learned about psychic attacks. She almost ran off the road when she glanced in her rearview mirror and saw him grinning at her from the backseat. She yelled at him, and he disappeared. Who was this guy, and why was he picking on her? Did he do this to everyone?

Exhausted and more than a little frazzled when she finally got home, she stared in disbelief upon seeing him sprawled out on her living room couch, grinning at her with his hands comfortably resting behind his head. She was already rattled by his wicked grin in the car, so this was far more than she wanted to deal with, especially this late at night. But her reaction this time was different. This time, she gathered her thoughts and confidence and blasted the entire home with a massive fireball of energy, imploring her guides to help permanently remove the intruder from her life. It must have worked, because she never had contact with him again.

She didn't understand why someone would want to do something like that. Was it to show how powerful he was? Was it to impress with esoteric knowledge? It didn't work; she wasn't impressed. She figured someone could find darker aspects of any craft, since any knowledge could be used or misused in helping others or advancing one's own agenda. But she had no interest in playing with fire. She knew that everyone astrally traveled almost every night while dreaming. She was pretty sure that was what had happened to her when she was floating in the violet. But the difference between a dream state and astral travel was that people who liked to consciously bilocate sometimes didn't follow any safety precautions, such as making sure they were still safely tethered to their bodies. She had once seen a client at a wellness fair who had difficulty in coming back into her own body. Olive and the other practitioners could tell she was trying to wake up after the session was over, but her facial expressions, rapid breathing, and growing anxiety showed everyone she was moving into dangerous territory. There were nervous discussions among the practitioners about what to do next. What happened if she didn't come back at all? Had they done anything wrong? Relief flooded the room when she finally returned to consciousness after about fifteen minutes, and then everyone just stared at her when she said she was trying to learn how to do astral travel. Olive and everyone else took turns explaining that there were safe ways to do it and ways that were dangerous. If one didn't want to do it safely, it was better not to experiment.

Another time, she was alone with a male client in his twenties who boasted about spying on unsuspecting friends and telling them the next day what he'd seen. She was sometimes baffled by the lack of ethics she saw in some people. She told him she thought that was morally wrong, and his response made it clear he saw no need to listen to someone he considered an inferior. She backed away from the table and watched in horror when she saw him move his body in ways that weren't humanly possible. First, he pumped his right foot so quickly up and down for twenty minutes that it became a blur. Then she watched as his body jackknifed, with his body and feet rising together to touch above the table. That would have been challenging for a trained gymnast, but then he did it again and again, faster and faster, for about ten minutes, until his body moved so quickly it was like the blurred foot. He had definitely picked up something—probably dark and probably on the other side—that had no intention of leaving. Did people not believe that horrible things could happen, or did they think they were somehow too skilled to be susceptible? She didn't know or care. But she still had an obligation to release whatever she could into the light, which she did. It wouldn't stop him from picking up new hitchhikers, though, the next time he decided to go flying through the cosmos.

When locking up a few weeks later, she and one of the other practitioners were both startled to see a ghostly image of a well-known community figure who had just passed away, leaving an enviable collection of antiques in his house. He begged Olive and her fellow practitioner for help, asking them to break into his house to retrieve items he didn't want his estranged wife and children to get when they sorted his possessions. Hearing both of them firmly refuse, he faded away, only to return a few nights later with the same request. Soon afterward, another practitioner mentioned to Olive that she had received a visitation from him with an unusual request. "Me too," Olive replied. Her colleague shook her head sadly; he had stressed the importance of a strong spiritual belief system, but obviously, if he was still so closely tied to all of his material wealth to the point of not being able to leave it, they wondered just how much he'd believed what he was teaching. That made Olive sad.

Chapter 19

Chakras

....

Olive and Artie had planned their dream vacation for the last six months, and finally, they walked into an oceanfront beach cabin surrounded by the Caribbean's crystal-blue water. All she wanted to do was meander on miles of white sand beaches; he was counting on enjoying the best seafood he had ever eaten. It would be a week of pure joy. Except for a nagging achy feeling on the back of her head, she was feeling fabulous.

But by the next morning, the dull ache had become a screaming pain. She hadn't had a headache since she was a kid, and she hadn't even brought aspirin with her. "It's not a headache," she kept saying to Artie. "It's more like pressure," but even as she said it, she knew that didn't make sense. "It's like something right at the bottom of my head is pushing out."

Artie was used to hearing things that sounded a little odd from Olive, but he worried that this sounded serious. Every day was an adventure, he thought.

They decided to stay in for the day. At least he could still see the water; she couldn't open her eyes right now. Maybe she was just unwinding from stress. Or she had pulled a muscle while getting her suitcase. She was frustrated that energy work didn't seem to help, even when Artie also put hands on her, but she also realized she had a hard time concentrating. He finally walked down to a small tourist shop and came back with a bottle of pain reliever. "Any better?" he asked as he got her a couple of capsules and some water.

"Not really, but these should help. I can't really explain it, but it feels like something inside is expanding. It's right between the base of my skull and my neck." The fact that they'd lost the first day of vacation was almost as painful as her neck.

By the next morning, the pain was still there but tolerable. It would be gone by that night, she thought. They both wrote it off as stress and started to celebrate their dream vacation on the second day. After a full day of sun, sand, seafood, and being deliciously worthless, she could feel the stress dripping off her like the garlic butter on the shrimp scampi. But by the third or perhaps the fourth day, an odd restlessness set in, and she started to search the area for other things to do, such as interesting historic sites or museums. She had nothing against tourist shops and margaritas, but after a while, they felt like cotton candy: they looked eye-catching and initially fun but ultimately left her feeling a little empty. They decided their dream vacation could also include side trips away from the postcard beaches.

She was surprised when the odd pain came back a few weeks later, this time even worse. The pain was in the same place as before, but the intensity had grown to the point of also making her nauseous. This time, she was pretty sure it wasn't stress, an allergy, or any of the other possible conditions she had already researched extensively. It didn't look like a cerebral hemorrhage, a sinus issue, or meningitis. She had never heard of a migraine being there, and she had never been in an accident. She finally agreed to have Artie take her to their family doctor, who, as a precaution, suggested she get an MRI.

"Nothing in the MRI looks like a problem," the doctor said as she read from the report. "Glad it's feeling better today." The pain was diminishing, but the concern hadn't abated. It didn't make sense. Why would this same odd pain appear for no reason? Now there didn't seem to be a medical reason for it.

If nothing medical was going on, she thought perhaps it was energetic. A few days later, while searching for nontraditional possibilities for pain in the back of her neck, she happened upon a reference to an emerging energy center called the zeal chakra. Her eyes widened as she read about the exact same experiences others were having. What was happening to her was also being experienced all over the world.

She, of course, knew about chakras; she had a shelf full of books on how the body received, interpreted, and expressed energy. Many people assessed wellness by using the traditional Hindu chakra system, which believed that each of seven primary energy centers coordinated a major aspect of people's relationship to themselves and their world. Chakra one, the root chakra, was located at the base of the spine and held the energy for feeling safe, having physical needs taken care of, and fears. Chakra two, the sacral chakra, was located in the abdomen and coordinated people's emotional responses to what happened to them (e.g., pleasure or sadness). Chakra three, the solar plexus, was located under the ribs and was responsible for identity, confidence, and self-esteem. Chakra four, the heart chakra, was located in the center of the chest and helped one connect to others as well the beliefs he or she held about him- or herself. Chakra five, the throat chakra, was located in the front of the neck and helped people to express their individuality, thoughts, and beliefs; speak their truth; and stand up for themselves. Chakra six, the third eye, was located in the brow and was the center of intuitive sight and creativity. Chakra seven, the crown chakra, was located at the top of the head and served as a direct connection to Source to access meaning and purpose in life.

As a teacher explained, "When any one of the seven chakras is not fully functioning, we often say that it is not in balance or that it is too open or too closed. When this happens, energy cannot flow freely through the body, much like an accident on the roadway can create a traffic jam. This can often feel like a part of our wellness is not accessible, such as with a lack of confidence or being reluctant to express what we really want. Tradition says that all seven energy centers must be fully open to enjoy happy, fulfilled, and productive lives.

"The skin is the largest organ in the body and is responsible for receiving all the sensory, emotional, intellectual, and intuitive signals constantly coming into us every moment of the day. Right now, your body is aware of your posture and your surroundings, your eyes are gathering written words that your brain interprets, and you are having an intuitive response to what you are reading. When a new signal enters your awareness, you either consciously or unconsciously respond to it. But if the energy center responsible for your reaction is not fully functioning, then you don't have the resources to take action.

"So why would a chakra not be fully functioning? Chakras operate similar to valves, opening fully in happy times to accept and store pleasurable energy. However, when we are disappointed, the chakra can instantly close for self-protection, similar to a turtle retreating into its shell. If you are a child who is often given hopes of going on a special trip, perhaps to the zoo, and then are consistently disappointed, with someone saying, 'Sorry, but I have to work,' 'I don't have time to take you,' or 'We don't have the money,' there is often a tendency to not want to open up and risk getting hurt again. Eventually, the child learns not to express preferences, saying, for example, 'I don't care what we do. You can choose,' and is often unable to express emotions. When this happens, we say that a chakra is closed, as in accepting defeat: 'I just don't have enough energy to meet this demand, so what's the use?'

"But it is also possible for the child to take a very different approach and perhaps not willingly accept a disturbing situation. When this happens, he may overcompensate by yelling, screaming, or having a temper tantrum. If he gets a positive response, then he realizes he receives benefits by acting out. The rewards are in return for an emotional outburst. Unfortunately, if this becomes the default tactic for conflict resolution, it's not uncommon for the tantrums in a toddler to create a drama queen in an adult. For this reason, people who don't have confidence may overcompensate by becoming bullies, taking others' power because their experiences have made them believe they are themselves powerless.

"Chakras that are out of balance can be restored by introducing a comparable vibration, which often includes energy work or yoga. You can also use a similar vibration of color, musical note, vibrational hertz, food group, mantra, or crystal. Only when all chakras are open and flowing can one truly find peace and wellness."

Olive now wondered what this zeal chakra was. She read, "Located at the intersection of the base of the skull and the top of the spine, the zeal chakra is also called the Mouth of God. As many people are starting to become more in tune with energetic changes on Earth, what is often called the shift, this center is starting to awaken from dormancy to help humans with what is often known as the ascension process. When fully opened, the chakra will help to connect to deeper spiritual truths, as well as to connect with nonphysical beings and other realities." As if to answer her unspoken question, she found one site that said that many years ago, everyone had had an open zeal chakra, but fears, both global and personal, closed it for most of humanity. As painful as the expanding pressure was, Olive felt she had just been given a gold star by the universe; the discomfort was a physical connection to her increasing spiritual growth. It had been uncomfortable, but now she knew why.

She would periodically ask friends and colleagues if they had ever experienced something like that and was surprised to learn how common it was. It seemed at least half the people she thought were on a spiritual path knew exactly what she was talking about. Their shared response was one of relief since they had been just as worried as Olive that there might be a serious health issue. But it was interesting, Olive thought, that the discomfort at the back of the neck was also experienced by those who didn't seem to be especially interested in their own spiritual wellness. She supposed the decision to be open to new spiritual truths was actually made by the unconscious or perhaps the higher self. Maybe it was the soul's decision; one couldn't just decide to call oneself spiritual because it sounded trendy. But there was also a pretty good chance that someone who wasn't interested in spiritual growth would never consider this option.

But if the zeal chakra opened with the help of guides, Olive wondered if they could also help with managing the discomfort. *After all,* she reasoned, *guides probably don't understand how a human experiences physical pain and instead only can understand its benefits.* So a few days later, when she felt the familiar discomfort starting to grow in the back of her neck, Olive asked her guides to please give her the gift in a way she could handle, maybe at night when she was sleeping or perhaps at a lower intensity, even if it took a longer period of time. She was astounded that the pain gradually receded right after she asked for help. That was the last time she experienced serious discomfort, although every so often, she would wake up with a slight ache in her neck, which then gradually disappeared. She assumed the guides were helping her in a way she could handle, just as she had asked.

She also recalled reading about another relatively new chakra called the high heart. She knew the heart chakra, located in the middle of the chest, was like the central clearing house for navigating relationships, feeling a connection to family and friends, feeling a sense of belonging and acceptance, and having a tribe. *It also coordinates how we feel about ourselves,* she recalled. *Do we love and accept ourselves, or do we carry guilt and shame? So if the heart chakra is the gatekeeper for connection to others and ourselves, then what is the high heart?* She realized it was the emotional relationship to Source, God, Allah, Creative Force, or whatever name one placed on it. She read, "Located a little above the heart chakra, the high heart is sometimes called the soul chakra, since some people believe this is where consciousness and your soul reside."

It was interesting to her that so many people were holding sadness in their heart chakras. Even people who outwardly seemed consistently cheerful were often storing something painful that had happened long ago. She could feel it immediately when she put her hands on a client, because a deep heaviness or grief was often mirrored in her own body. She was especially aware that many of her clients didn't appear to recognize the heavy sensation in their own chests, probably because it had become their normal. Maybe there had been so many disappointments and so much unkindness over the years that they had just stopped feeling altogether, protecting their hearts from further sadness. After the session, when the grief had been released, people were often surprised they could take a deep breath again. "My chest just feels so much lighter," they often remarked. Olive had read that holding on to persistent sadness could result in what was called broken-heart syndrome, at least according to medical researchers. In fact, not dealing with grief could often lead to physical cardiac problems, including death.

She never thought about her own death that much, possibly because she was still in her thirties and in perfect health, but she still got a little nervous when she started to have chest pains; then problems swallowing; and, finally, issues with her eyes not focusing well. Her blood pressure was normally on the low side, but every so often, it would skyrocket. Weird pains popped up, sometimes like a sharp stab and sometimes a dull ache. She was starting to feel like a hypochondriac with every doctor's visit. Despite all the EKGs, lab work, and testing, the doctor could find nothing wrong with her. She asked Olive more than once if she was under a great deal of stress. Yes, of course there was some stress; she was alive, wasn't she? If anything was making her even more stressed, it was all the weird health issues.

She was always tired, even after a solid night's sleep. Her blood work was all normal: no anemia, no mononucleosis, and no chronic fatigue syndrome—nothing that pointed to an answer. But why did she often feel as if she had been busy all night? In meetings. Going to classes. Gathering with others. Why had all her dreams become boring? It didn't feel like more than she could handle, but it was frustrating. She just needed more puzzle pieces to come together to have it all make sense.

Olive had often heard the term *ascension* in classes and discussions and was confused about the use of the word. Her only context was in biblical literature, as in Jesus's ascension after death to be with God in heaven. If people of all faiths and cultures were using the word, then how could they all be ascending? She assumed everyone was seeking to find peace and meaning in his or her life, but did everybody go to the same heaven? The use of the word didn't make sense to her. She finally realized the term *ascension* wasn't used with a religious connotation but in reference to spiritual growth, moving toward greater meaning and purpose in one's life. It referred to those who were having an awakening to new truths, new abilities, and new connections. It meant energetically moving into a higher level of awareness, moving away from materialism, fears, and pursuit of physical pleasures to an understanding in the oneness of all beings. It also could mean that all energy bodies—one's physical, emotional, spiritual, and mental selves—were merging into this state of oneness. It felt exactly like what she was going through: an intense period of spiritual growth.

She thought it was curious that massive changes were also happening right now all over Earth, including some so significant that international alarms were being sounded by both scientists and the general public: rapid climate change, earthquakes all over the world, supervolcanos showing signs of activity, and sea levels rising to dangerous levels. She thought about the ozone depletion; mass extinctions of birds, insects, and fish; the destruction of coral reefs and the Amazonian rain forest; pollution of the air, lakes, and rivers; and the huge islands of plastic floating in the oceans. It was almost as though Gaia were also having her own shifts. If Gaia was a person, Olive thought, she was probably pretty upset at how much people were abusing her.

Olive recalled hearing something about a band of electromagnetic energy surrounding Earth that was also recording significant vibrational swings. The Schumann resonance had been measured in multiple locations around the globe for about seventy years, almost always noted at around 7.83 hertz. For unknown reasons, it was not uncommon to now see spikes exceeding 50 hertz, or seven times the level of what had previously been recorded. In December 2020, it spiked at an astounding 200 hertz. She wondered, *What is the effect on our physical and emotional bodies with massive energy now bombarding us?* Perhaps there was a relationship between the rising Schumann resonance and why so many people now complained of experiencing stress, anxiety, and an inability to focus or sleep soundly. She understood what it felt like; it was almost as if one used to be caffeine-free but now lived on coffee and energy drinks.

She thought it was curious that the physical planet, the energy band around Earth, and many of Earth's inhabitants were all experiencing significant shifts at the same time. Was it possible that all the events were somehow related? Maybe the violence, anger, and disruption displayed by humans were somehow absorbed by Earth and the air. Or perhaps the physical changes in the atmosphere led to the anxieties felt by many people on Earth. *Since we humans are composed of the same basic elements as Mother Earth,* she thought, *it makes sense that changes in the atmosphere and deep in Earth can also be reflected in us. As above, so below.*

If the energy band was impacted by unknown forces, what about all the solar flares that seemed to be occurring more often? According to a NASA report, the sun will be rocked by an increased number of gigantic 'monster' explosions in the coming years.[1] Another site noted that so far, the massive solar flares hadn't directly hit Earth, but if just one of the coronal mass ejections had been directed at Earth, the power grid would likely have gone down and ended life as we know it. Something like that happened years ago called the Carrington Event. The massive solar storm knocked out all radio communications in 1859. *What might happen if a huge solar storm occurred today? No communications, no electricity, no heat.* She shuddered at the thought.

Olive didn't understand why everything seemed to be changing at the same time and wondered if there was a relationship. She realized how many shifts had occurred in her own life, mostly since the nighttime

---

[1]   https://metro.co.uk/2019/05/27/monster-explosions-sun-will-become-common-nasa-warns-9695956/?ito=cbshare.

visitations by the little gray people. She hadn't thought before about how many ways she had become almost a different person. She was becoming more open to different beliefs, less judgmental, and perhaps a little better at seeing how everything in the world—the people, the animals, and all of nature—all were part of one unified field of energy. Floating through the violet cosmos had made that concept even more real to her. She was less competitive and more forgiving. She found more enjoyment in the ordinary and spent less time being with people whose energies seemed incompatible with hers. She summed it all up with the realization that she was happier and more peaceful than she had ever been. If this was ascension, then she was loving it.

When she started to study what ascension meant to others and what it looked like in their everyday lives, she discovered that many books and websites included references to ascension symptoms. She read, "Sometimes the emerging energies can feel invigorating, stretching our imaginary boundaries with the new spiritual focus, direction, and abilities. New insights and abilities emerge: a greater sense of wholeness and connection and a deepening interest in creating a life based on meaning and purpose rather than money or power." She knew she was becoming more intuitive, but she never really had thought about how that fit into all the other changes in her life.

It was interesting that sometimes she went into periods when she was not tired at all, still wide awake well after midnight, and up with the dawn. Then there were other times when she could sleep the day away and still not feel rested.

But she also knew that stretching boundaries could be uncomfortable, especially if there was resistance to change or fear of where the change might take one. Sometimes resisting could look like physical issues, such as chest pains or headaches. She knew now that was what was happening to her: a series of odd physical issues that at first didn't seem to make sense. It seemed like a good possibility that they were all related. She suspected this was the root cause of all the weirdness she had been experiencing, such as discovering that the pain in the back of her neck was often associated with an awakening zeal chakra.

She started to make a list of everything that might be associated with ascension symptoms and was surprised at the many similarities she and her friends noticed. Everyone had at least a few odd health issues and sometimes more than a few. Just about everyone had gone to the doctor at one time or another and been told there wasn't anything medically wrong. Nothing showed up in lab work, so it probably wasn't an issue. Until all her friends started to share notes, every one of them had assumed she or he was the only one experiencing peculiar health events.

Olive wondered if humans' physical bodies were possibly recalibrating, similar to the global changes on and around Earth. She started to take note of the many issues her friends were having:

- fluctuating energy levels ranging from extreme exhaustion to almost manic energy;
- aches and pains, including apparent serious health issues, without identification of the reason;
- discomfort where the spine met the skull, in the brow, and in the heart center;
- an increase in dreams and meditations that appeared intensely real, including nonhuman beings or unfamiliar landscapes;
- changes in diet, perhaps avoiding meat, alcohol, or sweets or craving new items;
- awareness of different physical sensations in the body, including trembling, chills, uncomfortable warmth, tingling, vibration, ringing in the ears, or a sharp pressure at the top of the head or the back of the head;
- heightened senses, including intuitive ability;
- bloating or weight gain;
- increased awareness of the presence of nonphysical beings, especially around three o'clock in the morning;
- dizziness, occasional high blood pressure, blurred vision, mental fog, and difficulty concentrating;
- tension and anxiety with a sense that something important would soon happen or that one had a role in that event; and
- emotional changes, including depression, isolation, and sadness.

Knowing that others were having similar experiences made any odd occurrences she had much easier to deal with. They still weren't fun, but they were more understandable.

She still woke up almost every morning with a message or a face looking at her. Once, it seemed as though she could almost hear what the being was saying to her. She felt as if it were inside her head, since its mouth wasn't moving, just like the first time she'd heard, "It's time," many years ago. Even so, it was all still interesting. She also occasionally had the feeling Avratar was nearby. It was as if she could feel him, but they didn't talk as much as they used to. She assumed he was busy taking care of business on the other side of the galaxy.

But sometimes things happened that were more than curious; they were frightening. More than once, she woke up with strange marks on her body. Artie found fresh scratch marks on her back, as well as bruises, but she had no memory of having hurt herself. Occasionally, there were small marks that almost looked like puncture wounds; sometimes those would appear in pairs that resembled a bite of some kind.

She never had a feeling that anything bad had happened during the night, especially now that the night paralysis had stopped. However, something was obviously going on that didn't make sense.

A little while later, while she was receiving a Reiki session from Josie, the practitioner remarked almost casually that she had removed an implant in Olive's left knee. Josie didn't know that the knee had been tender for quite a few months; in fact, Olive had already had an x-ray and MRI to determine if the cause was perhaps something physical, maybe a torn meniscus. "Nothing abnormal noted," said the report. Not even arthritis. But amazingly, the knee now no longer hurt for the first time in ages.

Olive had heard about implants during her internship class but didn't know how to look for one or what it even was. Josie explained that the ones she had removed were the energetic ones; there were others that had a physical presence that could be seen in x-rays and even removed during surgery. She referenced Dr. Roger Leir, a podiatric surgeon who had written a book called *The Aliens and the Scalpel*, with photos of the dozen implants he had removed during surgery. Dr. Leir once had explained, "It is my opinion that someone, or some entity, from somewhere else, is implanting these devices into human beings so that they can monitor genetic changes which are occurring in the human body."

Another theory was that they were placed inside a person by extraterrestrial entities to influence them in some way. "Like a spirit attachment?" Olive asked.

"No, I believe that mostly, they are inserted inside someone who is awakening to stop the person's spiritual progress," Josie replied.

Olive wanted more information. She still was incredulous that her knee did not hurt at all.

"They can take any number of forms, from tiny, needlelike items to things that look like half-inch-thick rods that can be perhaps a foot long. Sometimes they look like tiny cubes or robotic insects." Josie said that to her knowledge, they were never for someone's benefit, and it would be a good thing to remove one as soon as a person saw it.

"But how do you get rid of it?" Olive asked. This was getting interesting.

"It's not like releasing an attached spirit," Josie said. "You can't encourage them to see a loved one or ask if they want to be out of pain so they will willingly go to the light. They don't have any emotions like a person does; think of them more like machines." She continued that sometimes a person could intuitively connect with them, which was how she knew that many of them said they had a targeted purpose. Protocol for the Center practitioners was to capture one and move it into the light, obviously with the help of guides. "Since they're like robots, sometimes we tell them they have failed in their mission not to be observed; therefore, their mission is aborted. Some people believe they are in contact with their senders, so we immediately try to isolate them, perhaps imagining a black tourmaline box surrounding them, before they are sent to the light. What is so interesting is that we have often seen physical issues resolved when they are gone—very similar to an attached spirit."

"So they can hurt you?" Olive asked.

Josie told her it wasn't uncommon to see a link to unusual discomfort anywhere in the body. "Like in your foot."

Or in a knee, Olive thought.

Then she wondered how long the implant had been inside her. Was it always in her knee, or could it move around? Was it always in the physical body or maybe somehow attached to the etheric field? Could it also have been attached to previous lifetimes? If her soul had a mission and the implant was in some way connected to her soul's journey, then maybe it had been with her for lifetimes. The possibilities were overwhelming.

<hr />

Olive was a little surprised that she still hadn't had her own Akashic records reading done, especially since so many of her clients had recounted past lives during their sessions. She hoped she and Artie had been together before, and if so, she wondered what their life had been like. Maybe she had lived in Greece or Egypt, places she felt seemed familiar yet had never been to. She scheduled a session with Laurie.

When Olive went into her session with Laurie, she was a little nervous yet excited about what she might learn. Laurie asked her if she had any questions about the records, and Olive asked her to explain them in her words.

Laurie said, "Your Akashic records are the records of your soul's progression since it separated from the oneness and became an individual soul. They contain every experience, action, word, and thought in all of your lifetimes, making them an amazing source of healing energy and information you can access to deepen your understanding.

"Some of the things the Akashic records can help you with are developing a deeper connection to your soul and opening yourself to divine guidance and wisdom. They can help you align with who you truly are as a soul and receive validation. Some people want to get answers to some of life's spiritual questions, such as 'What did you come back to this earth to learn?' and 'What energy are you here to leave in the physical world?'

"Many clients have questions about past lives, such as how those lives are impacting their current life. Sometimes we get information on contracts the client has created with other individuals, and we work on altering or releasing those contracts. In that same area, we can also identify and reprogram patterns and limiting belief systems that are no longer serving someone."

She chuckled as she said, "One thing that most people don't know until they come for a session is that they get a twofer. They get information from their records as well as their guides and other light beings. Sometimes we even get guidance from ancestors, and we are able to clear a belief or pattern in the client's lineage that will impact his or her ancestors and future generations.

"The most important thing I hope to do is to help you understand the possibilities that are your divine right. You can create the life you want—empowered, free, and filled with joy—if you choose to live consciously.

The moment you booked your session, your record keepers began working with you. They heard your pure heart's intention and began the process of readying you for the session."

Olive soon realized Laurie considered an Akashic reading a sacred connection to Source, not merely an interesting exercise. She listened intently as Laurie opened with prayers of protection and requested permission to enter Olive's soul's records.

Once she completed the prayers, Laurie smiled at Olive and asked her how she felt.

Olive replied, "Very calm and peaceful. I could feel the energy moving through me. I feel very connected."

Laurie told Olive she had felt a strong connection when she asked Olive to open her heart center. "It is very clear that healing work comes easily to you. You have been a healer in many lifetimes before this one. Did you always know you were able to help people?"

Olive replied, "I suppose that even as a very young girl, I knew I was different. I was so excited when I discovered my healing skills and learned how to use them."

Laurie said, "Your guides are thanking you and affirming what you have done in this lifetime. Many people ignore their gifts or avoid them. I know it must have been scary at times, but you should be proud of yourself for being brave and moving into your power.

"There is something else I feel now that I am in your records. Have you ever had the feeling you may have lived on another planet or in another dimension? It's very hard for me to explain, but I am asking the records for help and to give me the right words. Your energy is different from the energy of a lot of clients I talk to. I feel a little light-headed and—no pun intended—spacey. Your energy is wide open, and I see the planets and the stars, and I feel like my consciousness is expanded. Have you ever felt that way or had dreams of space-traveling?"

Olive stopped taking notes and stared at her.

"What? Did you think this was the only planet you had been on? Almost everyone has spent time in other dimensions or on other planets. Your soul can travel wherever it needs to in order to complete its mission, even on other planets."

Olive just looked at Laurie for a minute and then said, "As a matter of fact, I have had dreams about being in space, on different planets, and exploring. I thought they were just dreams."

Laurie smiled, told her she was an astral traveler at night, and asked if she ever woke up feeling more tired than when she had gone to bed.

Olive shook her head in amazement and then nodded.

"I don't want to startle you," Laurie said, "but you also have guides who are nonhuman shapes. I call them extraterrestrials, but they really are beings from different planets. All I can tell is that they don't look like us. Everyone has all sorts of guides—ascended masters, angels, saints, and ancestors—and you have a very large group of nonhumans. How do you feel about that?"

Olive responded, "That is pretty neat! I like that idea!"

Laurie then added, "Well, I am glad you like that idea, because your guides are letting me know they are here to help you with your purpose for this lifetime. They are here to help you be a bridge between our two worlds when the humans and nonhumans meet. They are coming to help us save our world, and they will need people like you to help the humans understand that they mean no harm."

Olive was incredulous that someone she had just met had told her the same things Avratar had said.

Olive had tried almost every service the Center offered. She understood how important it was to make time for herself; after all, wasn't that what she told her clients all the time? But when a client turned the tables and asked her what the one special thing she did for herself was, she had to pause to think about it. She loved to travel, but truthfully, she and Artie hadn't gone anywhere since their last trip to the Caribbean. She wasn't actually walking the walk, was she? Maybe she needed to do a better job of taking her own advice. She would talk to Artie that night.

They both realized that lying on the sun-soaked beach last year had really only been fun for the first day or two. When she had been younger, the only considerations for a successful vacation had been which beach, which brand of tanning lotion, and which drink to have nearby. She wasn't sure how to react when the truth hit her at some point that she was bored with the template that had been familiar but ultimately unfulfilling: beach, drink, shop, eat, beach, drink, shop, and eat. She didn't need any more clothes, she didn't enjoy the drinking, she had lost patience with sand in her swimsuit, and she was gaining weight. The "Beach, drink, shop, and eat" approach wasn't working anymore.

Fortunately, Artie was feeling the same unrest, so they decided to change the template, leaving the beach to move inland, exploring the local culture, history, religion, and customs of the region. Even months later, they still talked about visiting the ruins of early European settlements, the spectacular art found in churches throughout the islands, and the museums dedicated to the earliest native inhabitants dating to the sixth millennium BCE.

Looking back on that trip and stepping outside the familiar template of "Beach, drink, shop, and eat," she realized that was the beginning of starting to look at the world in a different way. It wasn't enough to live in the moment; she was driven to better appreciate every moment. She needed to understand how one person's moment could either positively impact the world or leave it an emptier place. Where did she fit into this equation? She was starting to see that it wasn't as important to read about a spiritual life as it was to live a spiritual life.

She had never before considered going on a pilgrimage instead of a vacation, but she was intrigued by one trip's intended purpose to connect each person to a higher level of meaning and purpose. It wasn't a religious retreat but more of a cultural experience. They put down a deposit and started to plan.

Studying spiritual and religious sites in France slowly shook her to her core. She struggled to comprehend the paths of pilgrims who dedicated their lives to their beliefs. She wondered how builders' faiths were revealed in the construction of shrines, chapels, and magnificent cathedrals. She began to feel the resolve and terror of those who understood they would be persecuted for their certainty. Maybe she was psychically channeling the unrelenting emotion saturated in each site, or perhaps she was connecting to something waking up deep inside herself. All she knew was that she couldn't understand why she spent much of each day wildly veering between deep introspection and a persistent sadness.

She was staring into a mirror reflecting her own beliefs, and she couldn't see the image.

This clearly wasn't a vacation, yet the trip became one of the most defining events of her life. There was little about it that was relaxing, yet it filled a part of her soul that she previously hadn't even known was empty. She didn't understand what had happened to her and was incapable of finding words to capture the confusion. She was living a life filled with a collection of things, a daily calendar of tasks to be ticked off, and people who bumped into her life like a pinball. Now the guideposts of what was known and comfortable had been taken away, and she wasn't sure what was left.

All she knew was that the trajectory of her life and an emerging belief system had been forever altered on that trip. She had thought she understood the concept of spirituality: finding meaning and purpose in her life. She could explain the concepts to others in great detail, easily clarifying the difference between spirituality and religion. "Religion needs spirituality," she would often say, "but spirituality doesn't need religion." But until that moment, she hadn't truly integrated the fullness of its message.

She didn't know who she was anymore, but she thought she had been given insight into who she was becoming. She was learning how to develop a belief system that worked for her, not one that had been handed to her by family or society and dogmatically followed. She knew that everything she believed was dependent on her perception, but that perception was often dependent on the information she had been given. What a catch-22.

She became conscious of a decision that would impact every aspect of her world: she was no longer going to live the life expected of her. She would live the life that felt right for her. *No one else can define meaning and purpose for my life, and no one has the right to tell me what I should or shouldn't believe.* There was a transformation taking place that not even Olive understood, but it was clear she would no longer blindly believe what others told her to believe. Actually, she was moving beyond belief to faith.

Faith was an even harder concept to deconstruct than belief. She saw belief as an opinion that was formed based on information, such as "Dark storm clouds make me believe it will rain." Opinions could change depending on new information received. But faith was based in trust, not information or knowledge. Sometimes that faith manifested in religion, and sometimes it didn't.

Perhaps this is a gentle awakening that comes with the eventuality of aging. The energy of youth is designed to navigate life's lessons. She realized that those who had already mastered the *how* of life often now focused on the *why. Why is purpose important? Why do we seek union with others who have similar questions? Why do we even have those questions?*

Many of those who had known and loved Olive for countless years were baffled by the changes in her. *But how could they understand, when they haven't shared my experiences,* she thought, *and I can't begin to communicate why I am different? Sometimes we know we must travel on separate paths; sometimes we share the same path we've traveled for so long with the awareness there are differences.* As much as she gathered her new experiences, she knew she also must release with some sadness parts of the other Olive that no longer fit into the puzzle. With every new layer and experience, she realized her beliefs were continuing to evolve. Some of those beliefs aligned with orthodoxy, but many did not. That was okay with her. As those beliefs continued to silently form and percolate to the surface, she hoped she would have the courage of a pilgrim to live those beliefs. *Heretics may no longer be publicly flogged or crucified, but seeking acceptance will always be a uniquely human trait.*

In a short five years, she had gone from her first encounters with gray aliens and an abduction to connecting with someone from the fifth dimension, night paralysis, Reptilians, spirit attachments, alien implants, and now a radical shift in how she expressed her soul, her spiritual self. She wondered where it was all leading.

Part of her couldn't wait to find out.

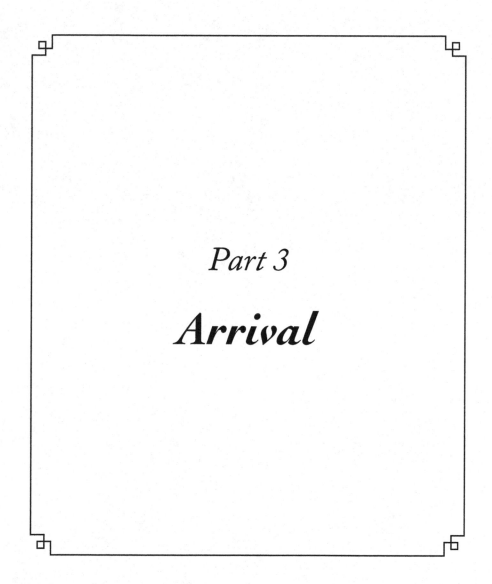

Part 3

Arrival

Chapter 20

Critically Important

·······················

"Good morning, Olive Stuart."

She snuggled deeper under the warmth of the blankets, returning the greeting with a little sigh. Stretching an arm and leg to the other side of the bed, she discovered they landed on an empty mattress. *If Artie already got up, then who—oh.*

"Hello, Avratar."

"Today I will answer some of your many questions."

She suspected that "Don't you need coffee?" wasn't on the list she had already started. She could smell the delicious aroma wafting up the stairs.

"You wish to know how to also connect with other beings."

That actually was on the list. She wondered when it would stop surprising her that he seemed to know so much about her. She wasn't even sure how she was talking to Avratar and was at a loss to figure out how to communicate with anybody else he sent her way.

It had taken a long time, but she finally accepted that this wasn't scary, and it wasn't all her imagination. He'd communicated first through a client, then Artie, and then with automatic writing. Now he was beaming directly into her. What an interesting life she was having.

She recalled that the first time a message had come through automatic writing had been in the office. She was certain she wasn't in control of the scribbles filling the notebook paper, as her hand seemed possessed by some unknown force. She marveled that her fingers seemed clumsy and unsure

117

how to hold a pencil or form a recognizable letter. The pen couldn't seem to stop at the edge of the thin horizontal blue lines, and circles were more lopsided than round. Something was definitely trying to connect with her; she just had no idea who or why. She threw out a quick protection just in case.

She had assumed that beings on the other side were omniscient and had mastered all of the human frustrations of life. Now she wondered if they also had a learning curve. Maybe it was just like kindergarten all over again, she thought.

It took a couple of attempts to decipher the first message in her office. Sometimes Olive assumed she knew what was being written and helpfully finished a letter or word. When the pen stopped its forward movement in silent rebuke, she clearly received the memo that the invisible messenger required no help from her. Patience had never been a virtue for her.

"Soon arrive."

Not only had she not written that, but she didn't even know why it was on the paper. She tried again a few days later and discovered it was much easier for both of them now. Letters were slowly and perfectly formed in a flowing script that seemed reminiscent of her early childhood. She wondered why someone chose cursive over printed words. She guessed it was probably easier than picking up the pen after each individual letter if words were printed.

When she asked who was contacting her, the word *Avratar* formed on the page. *Wow*, she thought. *This is so totally cool.* It was another physical connection. She wished it wasn't so important to have something physical in front of her, but for right now, that was just the way it was.

She allowed the hand to move freely without anticipating the results; the more she allowed, the more fluid the writing became and the faster the message arrived.

"We are coming to help."

She was baffled. *Why would they help or even want to? When are they coming? What could they possibly help with, and the biggest mystery of all, who is* we?

Sometimes the message was more personal, suggesting she take more time to meditate or perhaps eat more vegetables and fewer processed foods to keep her vibration as high as possible. During a late-night writing session, Avratar even once suggested that "the vessel" might be too tired to continue. She had to agree that her vessel was pretty tired that night.

"Yes, I think it's real," Artie reassured her more than once. "No, I don't think that you're making this up or that your subconscious is the one actually writing any of this."

At some point, he reached the end of his patience and finally snapped at her. "Olive, would you just knock it off? You're going to make them angry at you." It wasn't even his hand moving across the page, yet even Artie thought it was all real. She guessed she probably should stop questioning, at least for right now.

After weeks of handwritten messages in the spiral notebook, Olive was surprised to one day read, "Please use device on desk." The computer was the most obvious device in front of her, but she wasn't sure how this would work.

She felt a familiar tingling in her hands and then the slightest movement in her fingers. Then came tapping. Her eyes watched as the fingers flew across the keyboard. It wasn't so much that Avratar was typing as he was dictating his message. Words appeared in seconds on the screen. In fact, thoughts appeared so quickly that she just hoped she got the concept right, if not all of his exact words.

She was amazed at how the words flowed. Avratar spoke of the mission she had been selected for, how "critically important" it was, and how humanity would be helped. He said there were many around the world who were helping. "Many of your sisters and brothers in light are awakening. You are among those who will be working with us to help." She still didn't know how, but she was starting to see a much larger picture than she had originally conceived. She suspected it was a good idea to approach this whole helping thing slowly with baby steps.

Then they moved from single words on paper to typing to actual conversation, which was easier for both of them. Taking dictation still worked when there was something he wanted her to clearly remember, but dialogue was faster. In an odd way, she felt she earned his approval or gained credibility when she first demonstrated she could do it. She still didn't understand much about why Avratar had first approached her, but she knew she didn't want to be a disappointment.

She wondered if wanting to please others was a uniquely human characteristic. *If you make your bed and do the dishes, your dad is happy with you, and you get an allowance. If you do your homework and are not a troublemaker in school, you get to graduate.* She sighed when she realized she didn't want to disappoint someone she had never actually met, and she guessed she would probably help, even though she had no idea what she would be asked to do. Was there some kind of pathological state for people who did that, such as chronic people-pleaser syndrome? Artie would have been the first to raise his eyebrows at that comment; they both knew she was a pure Taurus, born under the astrological sign of someone who was more bullheaded than people-pleaser. Then why did she feel this was something she wanted to do?

She could usually tell when Avratar was nearby by a persistent buzzing at the top of her head. She waited for a few seconds until she felt they had connected. It was like the last tumblers falling into place on a combination lock when everything lined up.

"It is now time for you to teach others how to channel me and other beings."

He was the only one she had connected with so far; a brief flash of panic surfaced as she worried if she would be able to converse with other interdimensional beings. *Do they all use the same language? What if I don't understand clicks or sign language?* She wasn't even sure she really wanted to talk to anybody else.

She had been more than a little cynical about reading channeled books, even by the best-known authors. After all, it seemed easy to fake something like that; there was no way of knowing who was really legitimate and who was making it all up. Sure, the authors seemed as if they honestly believed the messages coming in. They talked about meaning, purpose, love, oneness, and all that, but what if it was all bogus? On the other hand, she reasoned, what if it really was all bogus? What difference did it make? The message was still the same, even if the messenger was making it all up. It was confusing. She secretly hoped they were all for real.

Except now she was one of the messengers. *Ironic, huh?* She supposed the universe had a great sense of humor. None of her friends or family understood why her new life was so important to her. She couldn't tell if they were afraid of natural therapies or what they might learn in the classes. Maybe they were convinced it was evil or wouldn't work before they even tried it. She recalled that not long ago, she had been firmly in that camp. Now she was channeling. She knew there were ample reasons to be cautious about even hinting that she was getting messages from the Great Beyond. She briefly considered mentioning it to her family at Thanksgiving, but seeing Artie's horrified look made her rethink that idea. They still thought anything that didn't come from the church was wrong—that was, anything that didn't come from *their* church.

She realized there would need to be discussions at some point, because now she was being asked to show others how to do it. It was better if they found out from her instead of a well-meaning neighbor.

"Olive, you will be aware of a different energy now coming into you. It will feel different from my energy. Do not be concerned. You are safe."

Suddenly, a little lump appeared in her throat, a slight tightening—not enough to frighten her but something she was aware of. Next came a little jump from her abdomen and then one from her chest area. Maybe she felt a slight temperature shift. She threw off the covers as a surge of warmth flooded her body.

"We are present."

"Who is *we*?"

"You may call us Marcus. We are a collective working on behalf of humanity."

In answer to Olive's unspoken inquiry, Avratar's quiet voice reassured her that he was also still present. "Do you feel the differences between our energies?"

She did. The one called Marcus had a slightly more electrical feel.

"We will be helping you to connect to the energies that will prepare you."

Prepare her for what? She didn't hear words anymore, but she knew something was happening all over her body. Her eyelids started twitching, and her heart was beating a little faster. She felt she was somehow receiving energy, as if she were being filled up, but she didn't know what she was being filled up with. Or by whom. She could still sense Avratar's energy in the background and had the feeling he was comforting her, making sure she was okay. She was just starting to calm down a bit, when her entire body started to shiver with a small vibration—slowly at first, with just a little tingling feeling, and then building to a visible shaking. She opened her eyes and watched her hands noticeably move. There was a brief thought that maybe she should scream for Artie in case something bad happened.

"Please know that you are safe. The transmission is almost complete."

She wasn't uncomfortable while the transmission, or whatever it was, was going on. In fact, it felt energizing, as if she'd just gotten a jolt of sunshine. She knew that didn't make sense, but she didn't have the right words to describe it. It felt—she struggled to find a word that fit—like happiness. But then the gentle shivering gradually slowed down and eventually stopped, and she waited for a moment to see if anything else would happen.

"Thank you, Olive Stuart. The transmission is complete."

What was that? she silently asked. *What did you do to me?*

"Your language might call it a download," Avratar replied. "It was to reconfigure your energy field to be in greater alignment with higher vibrations. It will be necessary for receipt of future communications."

"But how did you do it?"

"Your body has an electrical system that is configured for your body's lower needs. Humans operate in the third dimension. The beings you will be connecting with are from higher dimensions. It was necessary to give your system a greater capacity to receive from additional energies. You will see no physical changes. You may, however, feel as though you are more intuitive, more aware of emotions and events, as you are now more fully aligned with those energies."

Now that the shivering was done, she was actually feeling pretty good, filled with sunshine and soon, she hoped, coffee. "So is that why I am still seeing aliens every morning? I'm going to be working with them?" Olive's stomach still gave a little lurch at the thought, even though she tried hard to project confidence and self-control. She immediately got the impression she may have offended Avratar.

"It would not be helpful to call those who are coming in to help *aliens*. There are some who have an awareness that this term is not viewed by humans as a positive thing. You may want to call them simply *beings*. Some who will arrive will look more human, yet some will not. It is no different than saying that all pets must look like a dog. When a label is applied, you no longer see one's individuality. I can assure you that there are many, many individuals who are now traveling toward Earth to help. They may have different appearances, but they share a common goal."

Olive was still in deep thought when Starseed convened that evening. Marianne offered to channel Avratar so Olive could continue the conversation from that morning. The room was slightly darkened, and several audio recorders were in position.

"Why are there so many different kinds of beings?" She had lost count of the different species she saw. First, it had happened only as she was waking up, but now she got flashes of images throughout the day. Usually, it was when she was most relaxed during a treatment, but sometimes she would see something with her eyes wide open. Almost all of them appeared to have two arms, two legs, and a head. She saw things that looked different from her but nothing that was really scary. Occasionally, there was a tail, ears on top of the head, or three fingers. Sometimes the skin was smooth, scaly, thick, or leathery. Some were almost ethereal, as though she could see through them, and every so often, some seemed indistinguishable from those who lived on Earth. She wondered how many nonhumans were actually living among humans.

"You ask why there are so many different beings. How many different species of life do you have on Earth?" Avratar responded in a soft voice. "You will note that humans often have wide-ranging appearances according to their geography and culture, adorning themselves with various items of clothing or jewelry. Those who developed in the colder climates became fairer-skinned, with lighter-colored hair. Those who created the magnificent civilizations nearer the equator developed more protection against the sun's powerful rays. Some cultures originated the practice of extending their necks or skulls to designate beauty or wisdom. It is no different when cultures develop on other planets. Each has adapted to its own environment.

"Now consider how many species of animals, birds, fish, insects, and reptiles your planet also hosts. Does a snake resemble a giraffe or a human? Does a fish look like a butterfly? The beauty of diversity is represented throughout the universe, not just on your planet."

But a snake wasn't a higher life form, she argued.

Avratar's pause was a little longer this time, as though he were trying to come up with an answer she might understand. She slightly grimaced at the thought she might have offended him again. After all, he looked like an ant man. She mostly saw ants as insignificant, but really, didn't everyone? Maybe that gave the impression Avratar was also a lower life-form. Sometimes she felt as if everything she'd believed had been turned upside down. Would it be okay to say, "I'm only human," as an apology?

"Why do you believe that a snake is a lower life-form?" Avratar said. "Does a snake create territories or boundaries? Does it wage wars or enslave others? Do not confuse the human's tendency to control others with what you falsely label a more enlightened species. You recognize as truth only what you have been told to be true. Your adepts have often said that all forms of life are equally endowed by the Creator with the spirit of life. However, your mind does not allow for other life-forms to be equal to humans. Please believe that the human is not more evolved than the iguana, as that implies one is somehow better than the other. This is only your belief and the belief held by all humans, but this is not true.

"When you see the construction of cities or businesses, what you see is the outward display of technological achievement, the human's need to justify its existence and bequeath a legacy to future generations. It is to proclaim that you have a presence and that your worth is somehow linked to the things that surround you and that you possess. But truly, do you possess things, or do your things possess you?

"You are impressed with the brain's ability to develop complicated structures, but you do not yet see what is far more powerful: the soul's ability to weave an eternal web of connections that are more formidable than the physicality of your transient life. Your buildings will fall, and your civilizations will vanish, just as others will one day rise. What you perceive as having permanence, or even having value, is a false perception based on your need to validate your temporary experience on Earth.

"You value your worth in monetary terms. Those who make the most money or are the most famous are the most admirable. They therefore must receive the most happiness—is that not what you have been told? And yet is this truly so? Think about what brings the most pleasure, and you might think of a child's laugh, a sunset, or a kiss from a loved one. Humans have been presented the most priceless gift, the essence of the soul, yet you wrongly place value upon the most impermanent aspects of your lives. It is as though you have been given a precious treasure, and you play with the box in which it arrived.

"Each human is endowed with a gift of incalculable worth: a soul that only wishes to experience the beauty of itself and its connection to Source. In all of the universe, within every being and on every planet, there is only one thing that truly is eternal, and that is your soul. Unfortunately, your poets and philosophers perceive your soul as somehow separate from the body and mind, as though it is safely stowed away within a corner of your heart. Your religious leaders honor it most often when the physical vessel is failing, acknowledging its presence upon death of the body. And yet neither portrayal is true.

"The body does not contain the soul; the soul creates a body through which it can celebrate the magic of life. Your most precious manifestation of soul is how you bring meaning to every day and how you weave joy into every moment. The celebration of that gift is the reason your bodies have been created. Please know that it is not the accumulation of power and wealth the soul desires; it is the spiritual celebration of emotion, compassion, and kindness.

"When you share a joyful moment or assist someone in need, you also honor yourself through the gift of self-expression and self-love. Compassion and kindness are also a gift to yourself. Your own joy is enhanced. Think of it like nourishment for the soul and its expression.

"This wisdom has been fused into every cell of your being—a union of spirit and matter to glorify the soul's expression. It has never been a secret for only a select few to conceal from others. Many of your religions have created a mythology that holds that final judgment awaits each person by a Supreme Being at the end of one's earthly life. The ancient Egyptians believed your soul must be lighter than a feather, completely without sin or remorse, to enter the realm of heaven. Church leaders in the Middle Ages often sold indulgences to reduce the sins of your soul, a form of larceny that would lower the punishment they believed you most certainly deserved. Many have used fear as leverage to gain power and control, when the reality is that these scoundrels had neither the ability nor the right to claim jurisdiction. It is incomprehensible to me that the value of your soul could be so trivialized.

"Those who fly, those who swim, those who walk, and those who crawl are all equally endowed by the Creator with a connection to Source. You recall that you recently had the experience of being one with all of creation, do you not? You merged with the infinite web of the universe as you floated within the violet field of energy. You were gifted that experience to help you understand the unity of all life. Why would you not believe that each being on your Earth, as well as each being throughout the whole of the universe, also has been endowed with that connection and is also one with creation?

"Olive Stuart, there will be beings who will come to Earth from a great distance, using technologies that will seem incomprehensible to humans. You will be impressed by magnificent ships and awed by their marvelous abilities. That is, of course, understandable. But it is not their technological advancements you must focus on. Please place your admiration not on how they have arrived but, rather, on why they have arrived. Realize that you look very different from them, and you have a culture that is unlike theirs. Yet they regard you and all of Earth's residents as their cosmic brothers and sisters, sharing one life-giving essence. And much like how Earth families or nations bond together in a common goal, the occupants of the ships, the beings who are coming to help, are equally endowed with the life-giving essence of all life-forms. And they did not hesitate when asked to provide support to Earth's people."

There was a long silence when Avratar stopped talking. Olive wiped away a tear, and she heard someone sniffle at the far end of the room. Olive had never even considered how difficult this project must be for all of them, asking for and coordinating support from gazillions of miles away. Now those who somehow shared a soul connection with earthlings had left everything that was familiar to them to help those they had never even met. She suddenly felt very small.

"Do you have further questions, Olive Stuart? If not, then we will close for the evening."

They continued to sit in silence for a long time after Avratar left.

Olive never gave much thought to who would be arriving. She knew them only by the names for entire groups, such as the Grays, the Nordics, the Blue Avians, or the Reptilians. She tried to do some research on who they were but soon discovered there wasn't much agreement. One famous book said that an entire group was supposed to be dangerous; another website stated that a different group was supposed to be friendly to humans. She had no idea what to believe, so she figured she had to rely on what the experts wrote.

There were countless online images, but then she started to wonder where the drawings came from. Did everyone who put a picture on the internet actually see one of them, as she did every morning? Or did people just draw something and later slap a name on it? She inspected an image on one website that looked like someone she had seen just the other day, but the one greeting her the other morning had had a kind face. This one looked menacing. She started to also question where the information came from on those websites. Did the people who created the websites have personal information? *Because if I am actually talking to Avratar and all the others who aren't from Earth, then wouldn't I have the most accurate information? Why am I trusting people who have probably never even seen or talked to a nonhuman?*

Avratar had said the ones who were coming to Earth were like humans' cousins, separated by miles but sharing the same life essence. That made sense, especially since her father's brother lived six hours away, and they never saw him anymore. They were still related, even though there was such a huge distance between their homes. But it was an odd feeling to also consider that Blue Avians or Nordics could have personalities or families and that, for some reason, they'd volunteered to help. Now she had to consider that they also had souls. What she knew about off-world beings was mostly from movies or TV shows, and she couldn't recall watching anything that was favorable. Mostly, they were pictured blowing up the Empire State Building, attacking innocent people, or hurting cows.

But something didn't make sense. Every time she saw a movie or TV show about sending astronauts into space, it was always for a humanitarian purpose, such as to colonize planets in the Milky Way after World War III. Their purpose was never to terrify and conquer the residents of the other planets; it was for survival of humanity or even to be helpful. So why was it reasonable for humans to explore outer space on *Star Trek* but not okay for someone from Alpha Centauri to visit Earth? Captain Kirk, Mr. Spock, and all the others on the starship *Enterprise* were on a different planet every week, trying to help people who weren't human. At least on TV, the Earth explorers who flew around the galaxy were portrayed to be kind people, weren't they? If it made sense for astronauts to travel in outer space to help people, wasn't it just as possible that beings who lived on other planets could be doing the same thing? Wasn't it possible that those coming to Earth were just as compassionate as Captain Kirk and his crew?

She recalled a time in first grade when she was becoming friends at school with a girl who came from another country. Olive had a hard time understanding her sometimes, but they didn't need to talk much on the playground. Mostly, they took turns pushing each other on the swing and laughing a lot. She told her parents the girl was her best friend that year.

Then her parents met her, and she wasn't allowed to play with her anymore. When her friend hugged her during recess the next day, Olive ran away. Thinking it was a new game, her friend followed, until Olive whirled around and yelled in her face, "No! Go away! I don't like you anymore."

Stunned, her friend just stared at her with big tears spilling over thick lashes. Olive didn't have the words to explain why she couldn't be with her; she just knew people didn't like other people who were different from them. She didn't even know why she didn't like her, but that was what she had been told. She wanted to explain why this wasn't permitted, but it was confusing, and her friend wouldn't have known all the words anyway. For the rest of the school year, Olive often saw her sitting by herself, looking sad. Olive reasoned, "Well, it was her own fault for being different."

Now she was sickened by the memory and how heartless she had been. One day the little girl stopped coming to school, and Olive was secretly relieved she didn't have to see her anymore. It was just as well, Olive thought. *She probably didn't want to be friends with me either.*

Now here Olive was, years later, filled with guilt just thinking about it, knowing how much that experience must have hurt her. *I was just a kid and really didn't have a choice*, she argued to herself. But even then, she couldn't believe she had been so cruel and ruthless.

She wanted to find her to apologize, but she didn't even know her name.

Until Avratar had talked about how similar the other beings were to humans, she had never questioned the childhood experience or how her parents' beliefs might have shaped her own views. She had determined a while ago that she was no longer going to live the life that was expected of her. She would live the life that felt right for her. But she wasn't sure how much of who she was, and who she was becoming, was based on a belief system that had been formed when she was very young. *And what happens if that belief system isn't right for you anymore?*

She wondered if her parents' prejudices and biases had influenced her in other ways, perhaps more subtle ways. She assumed so, even if she wasn't consciously aware of the many possibilities. There was such a fine line between parents mentoring or guiding children to be little versions of themselves and allowing them to forge their own path. She was certain that not following their rigid beliefs would have been seen as a rejection of them. Maybe it was just to allow herself to feel less shame, but she reasoned that a six-year-old didn't even know she had the right to her own opinion.

She had won the battle not to go to their church when she was eleven, but that wasn't really because she was developing her own religious beliefs. It was just that she wanted to pick a battle to test her fighting skills, and that was the skirmish she picked. But in many ways, her parents had won the war. She still only bought a certain brand of cheese because her mother had said it was the best. She had avoided a certain neighborhood when house-hunting, because her parents had told her that something bad had happened in that area many years earlier. The list started to grow: *We celebrate holidays this way and not that way; we vote for these people and not those people; we watch these news stations and not those news stations; and people who come from these countries or who have these beliefs are okay, but the others are not okay.*

Soon beings who were probably very different from humans would be coming to Earth. She wondered how many people had grown up believing the same things she had been told.

She was filled with sadness as she once again thought of her best friend from first grade.

Chapter 21

Reptilian in the MRI

....

Olive continued to wonder how many of her beliefs could be traced back to what others believed. It was all about perception, she decided. *We all want to be included, to fit in somewhere. And if we can belong to something by sharing similar opinions, then we are somehow fulfilled.* Scientists had done a lot of studies on how humans made decisions based on what they heard from people they trusted. But what happened if their views weren't necessarily what others believed? How many people challenged those they trusted and respected, knowing that by doing so, they risked not being part of the in crowd? Why were some people seen as trendsetters and admired instead of ridiculed when they didn't follow the crowd? *After all, every single inventor or artist saw the world in a way different from everyone else, right?* She wondered what needed to happen to move the needle from one side to the other. *If you had two people who followed the proverbial different drummer, why would one be made fun of and one be famous?*

She was disappointed in herself with the realization of how much she had been influenced by her family and the church. If she had been so clueless about that, what else didn't she know about herself? Maybe there were other ways in which her opinions and behavior had been influenced or manipulated. She was pretty confident that her friends hadn't put any pressure on her, but then she remembered she had selected her college because a best friend was going there. She had picked her major because a teacher in high school told her she would be good at it. She'd stopped going to her favorite burger hangout just to please an ex-boyfriend. She'd started watching a TV show she secretly hated so she could be part of the conversation at lunch the next day.

Next, she started thinking about ways in which advertising also influenced her behavior. How often had she seen magazine covers that featured photos of pastries dripping in calories right next to articles screaming weight-loss tips to be more attractive? *What about all the commercials telling you that to be happy, you need to drink this beer or wear that mascara or buy those cars? The commercials must be successful in getting you to buy their products, or the companies wouldn't put so much money into marketing.* She remembered buying mascara she had seen in an ad but now couldn't recall why she'd purchased that brand. She made a mental note to check if her eyelashes were lusher, curlier, and thicker now.

She was starting to feel like a puppet. If she prided herself on being mostly an independent thinker, what about all those who had chronic people-pleaser syndrome? If their beliefs were based on what other people told them, how could they ever really know what they believed?

What about everything else that bombarded her with information all day long—billboards, movies and TV shows, news programs, and all the fundraising appeals that arrived in the mail? What about internet sites and social media, which either promoted the sites they wanted people to visit or blocked the ones they didn't want people to see?

Probably the most confusing of all was politics. Two people could hear the exact same thing and have two completely different views. Sometimes the ones who yelled the loudest weren't always the ones who made the most sense to her. It was easy to walk away from a discussion one didn't like; how could one fight a national policy he or she didn't agree with? She wondered if there was a national policy for how to work with visitors from other planets.

She thought a lot about her beliefs in the days that followed and was mostly comfortable with the opinions she formed from personal information. She knew which cities she liked or didn't like because she had visited them. When she had to rely on others for information or if there was something she didn't know much about, she usually put those comments into the category of "Hmm, that's interesting." That category seemed to be getting bigger and bigger.

She was becoming more involved in Avratar's project but still didn't know the specifics. He'd told her only that she had to prepare herself and that he was working on getting her ready. She explored parks with Max, Sophie, and Artie since Avratar had said that would help connect her with the beauty of nature. She read so many books that Artie had to help assemble another bookshelf. She never had enjoyed spending time alone, but now she was starting to crave quiet moments. If this was preparing her, she was okay with that.

She was curious about the differences in dimensions. She had learned in school that Earth operated in the third dimension, which meant humans functioned in three directions: length, width, and depth. If you drew a line on a piece of paper, you would have one dimension, which was length. If you turned the line into a square, you would add width, so now you had two dimensions. If you added depth by creating a box, it became three-dimensional. She supposed since humans and everything on Earth took up space, everything was considered 3D. Going from 2D to 3D was like watching a regular movie versus wearing the special 3D glasses that made everything jump out at you.

The fourth dimension was supposed to include time, but she got confused by the scientific explanations. Someone had said that ghosts were part of the fourth dimension since there was an energy imprint that was stuck in a certain time. Avratar had said he was from the fifth dimension, which was considered the beginning of the spiritual dimensions, since it brought in meaning, purpose, and compassion. Everything higher than that was completely confusing for her. She wondered where angels and fairies fit into this.

She was also curious when she would find out what she needed to know about the visitors. She still hadn't been told how she would be working with them. She had already seen dozens of different appearances, and the only one she had had a strong reaction to was the one that looked like a tall standing lizard, the one that had appeared after she had a few experiences with night paralysis. He probably was a Reptilian, because he had long claws, greenish-gray scales, and yellow eyes with pupils that looked like slits. Just about every website talked about how dangerous they were. She wasn't positive he had anything to do with the night paralysis, but she didn't want to have anything to do with him. She would rather get to know the ones with the kind faces.

A few weeks later, her left foot landed in a little hole while she was running, and by that evening, her left knee was swollen and inflamed. Artie packed it in ice, then a hot pack, and then ice again, but after several days, it wasn't getting much better. Nothing was broken, so an MRI was ordered to see if there was significant tissue damage. "You know how you always try to find the lesson in everything?" Artie said. "Maybe you're supposed to slow down." If that was the lesson, she was now moving as slow as Alice, her turtle spirit animal.

The technician slowly went over all the directions, gave her headphones to drown out the clicking noise, and told her several times that she would be safe inside the tube. Olive looked dubiously at the enclosed metal tube and asked what would happen if she needed to get out.

"Don't worry, honey." The technician repeated the mantra she had probably said a million times. "You'll be safe." She had straps and bean bags and so much bundled into the tight space that Olive couldn't have moved even if she'd wanted to. She guessed that was the idea.

She closed her eyes and tried to relax, visualizing a vacation, Artie, her puppies—anything but the inside of this contraption. Instead of seeing Artie's beautiful eyes, she was looking into yellow vertical slits. They were right in front of her on the largest, scariest face she had ever seen. He was huge, even larger than the one she had seen months ago, with a face so close that she could see every scale. She didn't know if she froze in place, since she couldn't move anyway. All she knew was that she was trapped in a round metal coffin with a dangerous Reptilian mere inches from her. What would the technician find when the table came back out? *What if I—*

Are you the one who is supposed to help me get back home? it asked telepathically.

She couldn't answer right away, probably because this wasn't what she'd expected. *I don't know how to do that*, she stammered. The immediate sadness coming from the being was so intense she started to get a lump in her throat. His yellow slits studied her intently for another moment, and then he slowly turned around and started to fade away.

But I think I'm supposed to learn! she mentally yelled after him. There was a slight pause in the fade, as though he were listening, and then he was gone.

Olive had no idea how long she was in the MRI after that. It could have been minutes or hours. All she could think of was how much grief she'd felt from him and how ashamed she was that her first thought had been that he was going to eat her. He had asked her if she could help him go home. Was he somehow marooned on Earth? Had a spaceship crashed, and he didn't have a way to reach anyone? How did he know she was someone who might be able to help? Finally, was that something she was supposed to do—help those who were trapped on Earth who desperately wanted to return to their families?

Only a few days ago had she even considered the possibility of off-world beings having feelings and families, and now the situation was just like some of the movies she'd seen but all switched around. Instead of humans trapped on Mars, here was someone trapped on Earth. And the sadness in that moment—it was as though everything changed for her. She had assumed the worst about him, and all he wanted to do was to go home. She had been trying hard to avoid being judgmental about people before she got to know them, and she had failed miserably. *This was some kind of test, wasn't it? Avratar wanted to see how I would react under pressure. I'll probably get fired now. I get the chance to prove I'm up to the challenge for whatever this project is, and I blow it.*

She hardly noticed her knee hurting as she limped back to the car.

"You did not fail, Olive Stuart. You had an experience that you had not prepared for."

"But what did he mean by asking me if I could help him get back home? Is that what I am supposed to do? And why was he down here? Are there others who are also here who want to get home?" Olive's rapid questions gave Avratar no time to respond. "And if I am supposed to help him, how am I supposed to do that?"

He waited until she slowed down to take a full breath before he responded. "There are many layers to your questions, Olive Stuart. We appreciate your willingness to provide support in our project. Yes, there are those who are on Earth who wish to return to their home planets. Most are here through unintended consequences. While that is not the primary mission of our project, this may very well be part of the process."

She pressed him for details. She had been patient long enough, and now she wanted answers. "What do you mean 'unintended consequences'? Was he one of the helpers coming in? I had a feeling he was trapped here. Why would he be trapped here? Why can't he go home?"

There was another long pause. She could always tell when he needed time to get the message right. Humans needed enough information for something to make sense but not so much that it was confusing. "Earth has always been a way station for travelers. Many of the travelers use Earth similar to a rest stop on one of your highways as they move through the solar system. Others visit Earth specifically to help humans or for other reasons. Some live within Earth, some live under her waters, and some live unseen among you."

Another long pause came. "In the distant past, the travelers would occasionally interact with humans. Ancient cultures would refer to them as gods and created temples and statues to honor their presence. When humans began to depend on the gods for daily answers and assistance rather than relying on their own gifts and abilities, it was decided that a temporary pause on traveler visits would be initiated for humans' benefit. Most of the visitors left at that time, but some were, sadly, left behind. Perhaps they did not return to the ships in time. Perhaps they had not even learned of the decision until it was too late. They will now have the opportunity to return home."

"But how did he know who I was and how to find me? It was as though he came right up to me, like he knew who I was."

"Your vibrational signature is changing. You recall that I suggested you avoid violent movies and alcoholic beverages? You now often spend more time in nature and frequently meditate, do you not? As your energies move toward higher frequencies, you connect more easily to beings in higher dimensions. In this event, the being identified your higher energy. It is similar to one of your psychic mediums being able to relay information from loved ones who have crossed over."

"But the person—the being—I saw today didn't appear dangerous. He wasn't trying to hurt me. I thought they were supposed to be dangerous. He looked scary, probably because I was surprised and didn't know what to do, but you told me to trust my heart, and my heart said he was okay."

"You must always trust your heart, Olive Stuart. Beings from other worlds are very much like humans. There are those who are more compatible with your beliefs, and there are those who are less so. Your heart will always show you the truth."

She thought again about her best friend in first grade. No, she hadn't been a bad person, but Olive had put a bad label on her.

Olive often thought about the contact in the MRI, especially about her reaction of immediate fear. She assumed that anyone, human or nonhuman, who'd ethereally popped into a meditation would have been startling, but the fact that it had been a Reptilian was especially confusing. Were they dangerous or not? The one in her bedroom certainly had looked threatening, but in hindsight, perhaps it hadn't been. Maybe it hadn't had anything to do with the night paralysis. Maybe it was just one of the countless beings who took turns greeting her every morning.

There was something about its being a Reptilian that seemed significant. She wondered if she would have been so obsessed with finding out more if it had been any other kind of being, such as a Lyran or someone from the Pleiades. She felt she had seen a Reptilian many years before, but she couldn't remember. Was that a memory, a dream, or maybe just her imagination? She had almost no recollection of her childhood, and she often wondered if that void was blocking something bad that might have happened. Artie could remember all the details of his early years, so why couldn't she? Whatever it was, she thought, she needed answers. She decided to get a past-life regression from Maddy.

Maddy explained that a past-life regression accessed the information in each person's Akashic records, the library of all of one's soul's journeys. Everyone had his or her own personal records, with all soul events connected to one primary mission or lesson that the soul needed to experience. That meant the information could come from lifetimes in the past or the future or from the current incarnation. Olive just wanted to know if she had had any other contacts with off-world beings.

Olive settled onto the massage table and listened as Maddy gently calmed her into a deep state of relaxation, deeper and deeper. She could feel her body on the table, but she also was aware of something hovering over her body that felt like a mist or a cloud.

She heard Maddy say several times that she was not her body. She could almost feel something peel away and slightly move toward the ceiling. Was that her spirit? It floated a little higher—higher and faster. Then there was no ceiling, and she was in open sky. Then the sky was gone, and she returned to the violet everything and nothing. How she had missed being there.

After too short a time, she was asked to slowly return back down to solid ground. Reluctantly, she obeyed. Maddy asked where she was landing, and she stated that she could recognize Earth below her. She floated to the ground and looked around to get her bearings.

"I see four or five large, powerful Reptilians standing together not far away. They're talking, but I don't see any visible signs of communication. Probably telepathy. They're ignoring me. Either I don't know what they're saying, or I'm not close enough to hear. We're in a large building of some sort, standing on an upper-level walkway, looking down at the main floor. Dozens of men are moving about, working with equipment of some kind. They're about fifty feet away. Some of them are moving things in boxes. It's a factory of some kind."

Maddy asked Olive, "What are you doing?"

She replied that she was just watching. There was a metal fence or railing around the walkway, and she had her hands resting on the railing.

"What do your hands look like?" Maddy asked.

That seemed like an odd question. She looked down at her hands. There were claws.

"Olive? Can you see your hands?"

She could, but it didn't make sense. "I have long brown nails, more like claws, on each hand. My hands are scaly and greenish. Four fingers. I can look down at my feet. Claws on each foot. My legs are the same color as the Reptilians. I'm a Reptilian."

Maddy asked her to observe what was happening and share whatever she wanted to.

"They're leaving. I'm still at the railing. They're the bosses, and I'm some kind of supervisor. I think they left, and I'm in charge. I'm smaller than they are. Not as tall or thick. Maybe I'm younger. I feel sorry for the people. They aren't treated well. I don't know what that means. I just know that somehow, I treat them different. If the bosses knew I treated them different, I would be in trouble."

Maddy asked her to go to the last day of the life. What did she see?

"I'm walking in a forested area. I'm old. Someone is walking behind me. She's female, and I think she's my wife. I find a place that has a depression in the earth, say something to the female, and lie down on the ground. My body is disappearing, disintegrating. It's gone."

"What did you learn from that life?" Maddy asked.

Olive was thoughtful for a moment. "I was kind to them, and they liked me. It was a good life." She worried about what had happened to the people after she left.

Maddy slowly guided her back to the massage table in the middle of the studio.

"I was a Reptilian?" Olive asked incredulously. "But how could that happen?"

Maddy explained that a soul could choose any location it wanted, as well as any form, to help its growth. "You've had your Akashic records read, right? You probably already discovered that you've been male, female, and every race on Earth. You just hadn't considered that you've also chosen to incarnate on other planets or in other species."

"But if we've all been Reptilian or Chinese or women or whatever, then we've all had the same experiences, and we're basically all the same, right?" As soon as she said it, Olive realized she'd just gotten another lesson in oneness. "And if we're all the same, then wars, hate crimes, and cruelty to others make even less sense."

Maybe that was another reason they would soon be arriving.

Chapter 22

Why Are You Coming?

....

Olive couldn't wait to tell Artie about her regression. He still hadn't done one yet. Actually, Olive sensed deep down that he would never do it.

"Really! I was a Reptilian! I mostly saw everything through my own eyes, so I never really saw my face till the end, when I must have been dead, and then I saw everything. I must have been floating out of my body. It was so amazing!"

Sometimes Artie felt as if he had a wife, and sometimes he felt as if he had a little kid.

"It was so cool. Only I was good. I mean, I didn't see anyone do anything bad to any of them before I took over, but I just knew they were mistreated. Want to get a regression done? Maybe we can find out how we've known each other."

No, Artie did not want to do a regression. Yes, it sounded amazing. He was glad it had been such a great experience for her.

Olive had asked Artie several times if he wanted an Akashic records session, a reading, or runic tarot, and he always said no. Sometimes he said, "Maybe someday," or "Not right now." She thought about surprising him with a gift certificate to nudge him along. Finally, she said with more irritation than she had planned, "I thought you believed it was all real. Now you make me feel like you think everything intuitive is made up and a waste of money." Olive felt his refusal to have an intuitive session was somehow a criticism of her, as if she were foolish for putting trust in intuitive wisdom.

He just stared at her with an exaggerated gesture of bewilderment, a big sigh, and his hands on his hips. "What are you talking about? I don't need to know if I was a tyrant in the fourteenth century. I don't care if I lived on another planet. And I sure don't want to know what is going to happen to me. I just want to enjoy what I have right now right here in this very minute. Olive, I think that every day is a gift to be discovered. That's why they call it the present."

As he turned and walked away, Olive heard him mumble that his life lesson was probably to have to deal with stupid questions like that.

Well, that was an answer she hadn't anticipated. So much for her intuitive abilities.

Olive checked off all the possible reasons she was wide awake in the middle of the night: she was not thirsty, didn't have to go to the bathroom, and couldn't recall having a bad dream. A cold, tingly feeling started as a hint at the top of her head, and then it became obvious. "Hello, Avratar."

"Hello, Olive Stuart. You have today received information about other incarnations, have you not? Do you have questions?"

"I do. So I think I understand the idea of reincarnation. But tell me—if I could be in another gender, another race, or another species, could I also have been an animal? A lot of people believe that's possible, but I can't figure out how that works."

"Your soul creates a vessel through which it can experience life. The consciousness you are obviously most familiar with is the vessel through which your soul currently speaks. The primary function of the soul's expression in the physical dimension is to gain insight for what it means to function in various capacities, which may also mean as a person, as a tree, as one who lives on another planet, or as an animal. For this reason, souls may select nonhuman entities if they so choose."

She thought about her three dogs. Molly had passed away years ago, and Max and Sophie currently had the run of the house. There was something different about each one of them. They all had their own personalities. Max and Sophie were more like Artie, living in the moment and happy to be doing whatever opportunity was in front of them: "Go outside? Yes! Something fun to eat? Yes!"

But Molly had been different. Was it possible for a dog to have not just a soul but an old soul? She had looked at Olive as though she knew more than a dog should know. It had been as though they were supposed to be together, as if it wasn't a coincidence that they had found each other again. When Molly had snuggled against Olive on the couch, there had been more than warm fluffiness; there had been an emotional connection. She'd had an awareness that seemed to include everyone around her.

Olive once saw a young child scream in fear when the big, fluffy white dog was eye-to-eye. Her mother explained that her daughter had always had a deep fear of dogs. Molly simply sat down, completely motionless, in front of the child. Within minutes, the little girl was hugging Molly's furry neck and asking if she could have her own dog.

One night, Olive was crying softly in bed after receiving a sad phone call. The unmistakable clicking of Molly's nails sounded on the wood stairs, and then Molly took a flying leap onto the bed, getting as close as possible, as if to provide the love Olive needed at that moment. How did Molly know Olive needed her? Molly was completely deaf and couldn't have heard a phone call, much less sobbing. Even more baffling, Molly had never before been on her bed, and she never did it again.

If dogs could have souls, then Molly definitely had one. When Artie moved into the house, he loved her as much as Olive did. In fact, they were inseparable. But then Molly suddenly left one day, possibly from a stroke or heart attack. Olive always wondered if Molly came into her life as a protector and turned the role over to Artie when her job was done.

Olive told Avratar that she didn't completely understand the whole concept of souls, but that was okay. Lately, there was a lot she accepted without fully understanding.

"Avratar, I understand that the term *ascension* means there's a growing spiritual awareness, like an evolution. I used to think it only meant something religious, but I don't believe that anymore. I can tell I'm different somehow, so maybe I'm moving in that direction. I don't know. I hope so. But is it possible for the whole planet to also ascend? I know that probably sounds ridiculous to you, but it feels like Earth has her own soul or personality or something."

"Why do you think about this, Olive Stuart?"

"I don't know. Ever since we were talking about animals having souls, I've been thinking about what else might have a soul. I keep thinking about Gaia and how upset I would be to have my beautiful rain forests destroyed, pollution in the oceans and the water, and all the violence. I think about all the dolphins, whales, and birds that seem to just die all at once all over the world. Now I've been reading that forty percent of the world's insect species are moving toward extinction. I feel like I should apologize to her for what we have done to her. Is that stupid?"

There was a long pause. Olive knew that what was coming next was important.

"You are perceptive, Olive Stuart. Gaia's soul created this planet at the dawn of time, and she has witnessed many changes over the years. She is the guardian of mountains and meadows, as well as all forms of animal, mineral, vegetable, and human life, and she dearly loves this planet and all that is upon it. However, she has become greatly saddened by what she is witnessing. Humans have only been on this planet for a relatively short amount of time, yet the damage that has been inflicted on her is significant."

There was another long pause. "Gaia has provided warnings of her displeasure for many years, and now you see signs of her awakening and taking action. Storms are becoming more destructive, hundred-year floods are becoming commonplace, and devastating earthquakes are now being experienced all over the globe. Volcanoes, including many your scientists have termed supervolcanoes, are signaling that they are now becoming active. Should they become fully awake, there will be significant impact. Viruses that at one time were manageable through the use of medicines are no longer capable of having their spread restrained.

"At one time, the harm to your Earth, water, and sky might have been reversible. Messengers have often forewarned your leaders of Earth's potential fate, yet their alarms have been scorned and dismissed. Those who honor money and power at the expense of Gaia's treasures have chosen a dangerous path for humanity.

"I recall a time when humans lived in harmony with the natural world. They honored what Earth provided and thanked Gaia for sharing her bounty. Now humans no longer give gratitude and instead plunder her limited resources for selfish objectives. The poisons that are poured into her soil are also polluting her waters and sky. Your grains, fruits, and vegetables no longer have the life essence they once did. Your fish absorb the chemicals spilled into the oceans, lakes, and rivers, thereby transporting toxic substances into your bodies. There are large expanses of your oceans that now can no longer harbor life. Soon Earth itself will no longer be able to support life.

"There are consequences to this sustained assault on Gaia. You may not see the decreasing protection of Earth's protective ozone layer, but the effects are becoming manifest. Glaciers and rain forests are disappearing, and with that disappearance comes the destruction of wildlife in those areas. Rising ocean temperatures mean the magnificent water creatures are losing their food supplies and breeding grounds. Coral reefs are disappearing, threatening the fragile balance of life within their waters. Sinkholes and massive gashes in Earth's surface are changing her topography.

"You no longer live peacefully with your neighbors and have instead created cultures of fear and mistrust. Those who have the most destructive weapons are viewed as the leaders. Cruelty to others is no longer considered an abomination. Ridicule, dissension, and conflict are acceptable; those who maintain a more peaceful way of life are considered weak. And those whom society proclaims as the moral leaders of your culture are often the greatest perpetrators of violence, discord, and maliciousness upon others."

Now it was Olive's turn to be quiet for a long time. "Avratar, are you saying the beings will be coming in to help fix the problems humans have created?"

"In a manner of speaking, yes."

"How will they do that?"

"The specifics need not be addressed at this time. But you have an understanding of the importance of this project. There are many individuals on your planet who wish to live in harmony with the planet and each other, yet they are denied this opportunity. That was not the original intention for this planet. The injustices and the continuing harm to Gaia will not be permitted to continue."

Olive listened intently, but something didn't make sense. It wasn't that she thought Avratar wasn't telling the truth as much as she felt he wasn't telling the whole truth. He was consistent in that he gave her only the information he thought she could handle, but she felt she was at the point where she could handle more. She had gotten pretty good at trusting her instincts, and she was sure there was an important piece missing. In every discussion about the arrival of light beings, there was a sense of urgency and something that seemed personal for Avratar. She believed that long-term consequences to the environment were inevitable if something wasn't corrected, but like most people, she figured humans probably still had time, and eventually, scientists would find a solution.

Then another puzzle piece fell into place, and she said, "But there's more to this, isn't there? If something isn't done, then something bad could happen that involves the ones who are coming in, right? Maybe even you. That's why I keep feeling that this is very personal for you."

There was another long pause. "You are correct, Olive Stuart. There is a consideration that I have not yet mentioned. We have discussed previously that I am from the fifth dimension. This is an energetic field with a vibration that is on a different frequency than your reality. Think of this not as a different location but as a different vibration, which means the fifth dimension is not bound by the physicality of your density."

She always had a hard time following Avratar when they talked about dimensions, but she could tell this was something important, so she needed to focus. "I think I understand."

"Think of dimensions like layers of thin cellophane, with one dimension stacked upon the others. In this example, the stacked layers would have almost no thickness. So if you looked at the stack of layers from the side, you would have an awareness that the third dimension, the one in which you reside, was one of the layers, but probably you would not be able to clearly identify it. But if you looked down on the stack from the top, you could clearly look through each layer. You would first see items on the upper level of the stack, then those below, and possibly many levels below that. One of the layers would be yours. Does that make sense?"

Sort of, she thought.

He continued. "There are many beings who call these dimensions home. Some of us operate energetically close to yours in the fifth dimension, and many others operate in higher dimensions. Those many dimensions are now threatened by the actions of humans."

There was another long pause. "At the end of your World War II, there were two atomic bombs detonated. Those bombs did significantly more damage than human eyes would have seen, as the most contemptible harm was done to those whose only interest was to live peacefully in other planes. And now there are in excess of fifteen thousand nuclear weapons on Earth, in the hands of a small group of governments. Each of those governmental entities believes its supreme power lies in the threat of destroying other governments, yet there is little or no awareness that detonation could ultimately destroy themselves or even your entire world. The quantity of nuclear weapons could easily eliminate all life on Earth seven times over. And it could also ultimately destroy the multiple dimensions in which we operate.

"Beings from other planets and dimensions have visited Earth since its formation billions of years ago, with most of the beings honoring the universal request for noninterference in Earth activities. Your planet's use of nuclear weaponry now mandates an intervention. This is not the first time Earth's people have experimented with destructive technology. You may have an awareness of Atlantis, the nation that disappeared below the waves many years ago."

The puzzle pieces were starting to come together for Olive. "So if a nuclear weapon was launched toward one country, that country could fight back by launching its own weapons. And then even more missiles could be involved. Maybe it would be like a row of dominoes, and before you know it, the entire planet could be impacted. We could even destroy the whole planet."

Then she realized that every explosion could harm more than Earth people. If there were civilizations who lived in other dimensions, then all of the conflicts on Earth would hurt them. It was starting to make sense. The stupidity of a few people on Earth could cause devastation for countless beings who only wanted to help.

"Your statement is close but not completely accurate, Olive Stuart. It would be more accurate to say that use of nuclear weapons would completely obliterate those dimensions."

The magnitude of what he was saying was making her feel light-headed. She suddenly understood why there was such a sense of urgency. Many countries were stockpiling weapons and making threats. *If only one of them decided to attack ...*

"Furthermore, there is now a fragile balance within your solar system. Your planets have a well-designed revolution around your star, which you call the sun. Moons, asteroid belts, and comets all move within a well-ordered web of energy pathways. Established movement of each sphere within the solar system is dependent on the location, movement, and gravitational field of the other spheres. It is the totality of this fragile balance that is, in fact, imperiled.

"Think about your games in which you stack cards to make intricately designed structures. Or creating a mobile that is perfectly balanced according to the weight on each side of the hanger. Now visualize removing a strategic piece from your design. What do you think would happen to your creation's fragile balance?"

The image of a house of cards falling into chaos was immediately followed by the horror of what might happen to the entire solar system if Earth was destroyed. The gravity of the situation hit her hard. No wonder there was a sense of urgency. She didn't know how much more she could take, but Avratar continued.

"There is one final consideration, Olive Stuart. Your Earth has had countless civilizations during the previous millions of years of Earth history, with many of them attaining a superior level of technological achievement. This fact has been hidden from you and all people of Earth. We have spoken about Atlantis, but there have been many other advanced cultures on Earth that predate your known history. The introduction of technology was initially viewed as a benefit to the residents of these other civilizations, and in many cases, this was true. Machines replaced backbreaking labor, assembly lines manufactured goods at an unprecedented rate, and mechanized transportation revolutionized mobility.

"But in every case, the increased integration of machinery further into the lives of the citizenry significantly changed their connection to each other, to their communities, and to their world. Communication, information, and entertainment now were through devices rather than contact with other beings. Technology advanced to the point that beings were dependent upon their machinery. The next step in development was the physical union of machinery into a being. Initially, it was the replacement of a joint or limb with a mechanical structure to assist with mobility. Then came placement of pacemakers and other machines to aid in daily function and, finally, the implantation of electronic devices within the organic being to impact cognition. It was this final step that would predictably prove to be each civilization's ultimate undoing. This progression has been repeated throughout time and countless civilizations with the same results.

"At one point, humans controlled their technology; now humanity is facing the real prospect of technology controlling you. Technological development now makes it possible to implant chips in the body to unlock electronic doors and purchase coffee. People marry holograms, carry robotic babies, and prefer mechanical dogs to the real ones. Cars are self-driving, and supercomputers can now calculate in seconds what would previously have taken decades. Robots are so lifelike that one has been granted full citizenship by a country. Computers are now capable of designing their own algorithms, effectively creating stronger and more powerful versions of themselves completely independent of their human creators. What was initially believed to be a benefit for humanity will ultimately replace humanity.

"It has been projected by leaders of your technologies that within a few short years, the human brain will be fully computerized. This surprises you? Yes, your brain will be replaced by a computer. When that happens, the human will cease to exist, and you will live in a world of mechanized androids.

"The youngest members of your world are enthusiastic about playing video games in their mind and conjuring information or making a phone call with merely a thought. They have been seduced by the possibility of unlimited powers, and they will transform willingly into avatars of themselves. What they have not been told is that there is a price for their entertainment. And that price each must pay will be to exchange humanity for becoming automated.

"What does this mean? When humans accept the appeal of unlimited data and implanted cognition, they will lose their connection to all that it means to be human. You will no longer feel emotions, which is the most treasured part of being human. You will become a machine. Many will not see the concern in this, as they will not even have an awareness of the gradual encroachment of technology on all of humanity. When the transition is completed, humanity will cease to exist."

Avratar had mentioned when she first met him that he once had experienced life as a human. He hadn't explained more than that, and Olive hadn't thought to ask. But now she wondered if that was why he had been selected, or perhaps volunteered, to be her contact. Maybe it had something to do with emotions. She heard a deep sadness in his voice as he continued.

"What makes a human so unique? Your emotions and your soul, both of which are lost in the transition to mechanization. We have witnessed this time and again in other civilizations. Some of the travelers who have volunteered to help humans are those who now regret the enslavement of their own minds by rampant reliance on technology. They will come in the hope that their stories will benefit those on Earth. There may also be a hope that they may recover something lost.

"Humanity is unique in our galaxy, which is why so many of us have monitored your progress and are so fearful for your planet's probable downfall. There was so much hope that you would not succumb to the same fascination with artificial intelligence that others have experienced."

There was another long pause. Olive's heart was racing. She kept thinking of the adage to be careful what one wished for, since now she had no idea what to do with this information. This was much bigger than she ever would have believed. But it all made sense now—why they were coming in and why their project needed to happen soon. Everything he said felt real. Not only did she finally grasp the urgency, but now she had a different awareness of the mission's significance.

Avratar's words now came out much more slowly, as though every word were carefully selected. She had the feeling he was preparing her for the most important part.

"The appeal of computerized cognition has been propagandized by those who would most benefit. This is not a haphazard or unplanned insertion into humans' lives. Your scientists did not have the awareness or skills to initiate a worldwide transition to human-machine integration." There was another pause. "You and I have spoken before about beings who are positively aligned with humanity and those who advocate a different agenda. We have encouraged you to discern which beings are helpful and which may not be.

"Earth and her humans are of great interest to many visiting groups for different reasons. I have stated that there are many beings monitoring Earth and its residents. But we have not previously spoken about the fact that many of those who are now present and who will be arriving do have a competing agenda. It is in their interest to encourage alliances that are not beneficial to humans."

Olive finally broke her thoughtful silence by asking, "Are there beings—I'm going to call them negative ETs—that are here to hurt humans? And if so, why? What do they have to gain?"

"There is only one thing in the entirety of the universe that is eternal and cannot be created or destroyed. Stars come into creation and can be extinguished. Planets, as we are now discussing, can be destroyed. But this one item is truly the most prized and the only timeless entity in existence. Do you know what that is, Olive Stuart?"

It only took a moment. "Your soul! It's the battle for our souls, isn't it?"

"Your world traditions all have stories about making a deal with the devil and selling your soul for something you recklessly believe is more valuable. In your trade, you receive what you most desire, perhaps money, youth, or power. However, you foolishly exchange something that represents eternal wealth for something of transient value. The Buddha, the Bible, and the ancient Jewish texts all speak of the soul's battle with evil.

"There are those who crave the immediate gratification that artificial intelligence can often provide. Your video games and movies entice with imaginary players demonstrating magical powers. It is a fancy that lures an ordinary person into believing he can transform into a superhuman. With the introduction of so many electronic devices, your culture has already moved from living in community to living in isolation. You talk into boxes instead of each other's faces. You have devices in your homes and cars that will respond to your orders. Taking the final step to full automation is an easy choice for those who are already feeling disconnected from others.

"Your poets, artists, and spiritual leaders speak of the soul as your eternal connection to Source. Some call this a union with the universe,

God, Allah, the divine, or Creative Force. The name is not important. What is important is the everlasting connection to the supreme life-force energy. When you choose machinery to automate your life, you voluntarily release the honor and privilege of having soul as your primary essence. Those who choose machinery over spirit will never be able to reclaim that former bond."

"So what happens to them?" Olive was frantically thinking about who might be in that category. A nephew who was addicted to online video games. A family in a restaurant who stared continuously at their phones during dinner. A man who started his motorcycle just by waving a hand containing some kind of implanted chip. Someone who'd inserted some kind of turbine that one could actually see rotating in an artery in his forearm—the blood flowing through the little machine powered all of his other implanted devices. There was already something called a neural implant that connected one's brain directly to a computer. He was right; there would be a lot of people who wanted a computer for a brain. "What happens to the people who give up their soul?"

"There are many layers to your answer. Your religions exist for the primary purpose of urging one to live an exemplary life. Many teach that the final judgment of your life's deeds is solely by God, and there are only two options: the promise of everlasting joy in heaven or the threat of eternal damnation in hell. Every religion believes that voluntarily rejecting their sanctioned beliefs, in effect following the devil's path, will bring horrific consequences for all time.

"The reality is far more complicated, Olive Stuart, for it is not the divine that judges you but you yourself. Each soul, your soul, is without ego, without an awareness of self, because there is no individual self. There is only oneness and being part of the essence of divine union. For this reason, your soul can be objective in what it determines it needs to learn to continue its evolution.

"Perhaps you recognize that you exhibited a pattern of being unkind to others. Your soul might determine that it needs to learn compassion, so it might create learning opportunities to do so in a future incarnation. Your soul could choose a body that had physical or mental limitations. You may find yourself homeless and reliant on the kindness of others to survive. These experiences present opportunities for growth; you have the free will to understand the lesson or choose not to. If the lesson is not learned, you may create additional opportunities in future incarnations. Those who have chosen a path of persecution, illness, or adversity have not created punishments for themselves but, rather, growth opportunities for the soul to further expand its awareness.

"This is the foundation of the law of karma, a balancing to help develop a deeper understanding of all phases of human personality. Unfortunately, there are many on your planet who misunderstand the concept and instead see karma as punishment or retribution. This is a sadness, as the soul itself has chosen what it most needs to understand to progress its wisdom.

"You asked what happens to those who give up their soul. Perhaps you have seen individuals who appear to have what might be called dead eyes or soulless eyes. They no longer have the divine life essence within them. They will never again experience pain, but they will also never again experience joy. This is because they will never again experience anything. They are similar to what you might term a *zombie*. Some who are lost are easily identified by their totally black eyes. Should you have contact with one, perhaps if one asks to enter your house or car, I suggest immediately refusing and locking your house or vehicle for your protection.

"Let us return to those you have termed *negative ETs* and their interest in human souls. Humans have yet to discover how powerful your souls truly are. Science notes that humans only use about five percent of their brains; however, science does not have the ability to measure the astonishing power of their souls. Those who do understand and believe in their own power can truly accomplish miracles.

"Everything in this vast universe is composed of Source energy. Consider the power of your sun and the countless stars that create the brilliance of constellations. Now think of all the planets circling each star and all of their beings, vegetation, water, and rocks. Can you imagine how much energy is flowing? Now realize that everything between every sun, every planet, and every asteroid, the void that your scientists term *empty space*, is actually a vibrational field that is pulsing with life. Again, your science does not have the capacity to measure the magnitude of this electrical field.

"Now realize that your soul and the electrical field are one. You are the field. You are the sun, the moon, and the planet. You are the field of energy pulsing with life among the stars. It is not that the field is contained within you; rather, it is inseparable from you. You are far more magnificent than you can imagine. And you know that you are far more than your physical body.

"Now that you have an awareness of the soul's power, realize that there are also others who not only know about this power but also seek to use this power for their own purposes. They see your soul as a commodity, much like coal or oil, to be harvested for the energy it produces. There is indeed a battle coming, Olive Stuart, but it is a battle fought for your soul. Beings who have loved and monitored Earth's creatures since the beginning of the grand experiment will not allow our most beloved sisters and brothers to be drained of all that makes them human.

"This is why we will come to protect and defend our precious brothers and sisters and safeguard all that is human. And that is why we need your help."

Chapter 23

Your Help Is Needed

....

If any of her friends had told her they were in conversations with multidimensional and extraterrestrial beings who were now on their way to planet Earth to help humanity, there was no doubt in her mind she would have rolled her eyes. Even with all that had happened to her in the past few years, she still would probably have had a hard time believing an outlandish story like that. Yet she was certain that everything he had shared was true.

But Olive was still thoroughly confused. "I'm really sorry, Avratar, but I just don't understand how I can possibly help you. I really do believe you when you talk about the entire planet going through something huge. Maybe even the entire universe. But how can I possibly provide any help?"

"You now have an awareness that this is not an insignificant project. There are many nonhuman beings who have offered to assist in various capacities, but we all share one common goal: to prevent Earth's self-destruction. This is not unlike the leader of a country sending troops to a neighboring country to provide humanitarian aid in a natural disaster.

"Every team of volunteers has accepted a specific challenge to help resolve Earth's problems. But with all of our technical skills, there is one responsibility we are not able to fully accomplish, and that is our ability to effectively communicate our intentions to Earth's people. Humans will see our ships above them and will have questions."

"Questions? They'll have a lot more than just questions," Olive said. "They'll be terrified. Do you have any idea how many horrible sci-fi movies for the past seventy years have shown flying saucers blowing up cities?"

"Yes, sadly, I do know. Which is why I would like your help. Unfortunately, the representation we have had in your movies is inaccurate. People need to know we are not coming to frighten or harm anyone. We are coming to help. It is not our intent to create concern. We need you to please inform Earth's citizens of our intentions."

Olive closed her eyes and tried to take deep breaths. He might as well have asked her to arrange for world peace before they arrived, just to make their job easier. Olive felt helpless. Did he not realize how impossible that was? Did he think she could just send a press release to the TV networks, and everyone would suddenly be grateful for the news tip? "Thanks, Olive! We'll run this as our lead story!" Or maybe she could just call the secretary general of the United Nations and ask him to take care of it?

"We ask you to write a book. They will need to know why we are arriving. Tell them that our intention is to help humans."

"Why me? What would I say? How would I convince them? I don't know anything about writing a book," Olive said. "Why would anyone even listen to me?"

"They will listen because you will be offering them the truth. Tell your story," he said. "They must understand that we are here to help. Time is limited, Olive Stuart."

She thought about what had happened during the past year when she'd told just a few people of her experiences with Avratar and all the messages she was receiving. She had thought that friends and family would be intrigued by her stories. She had been sure that not only would they be happy for her, but some probably would also be envious. Even if they didn't share her excitement, she had thought, at the very least, they would pretend to be interested. But that wasn't the way it had happened. She was still hurting from the jokes and snide comments.

But now, for the first time, she understood their reactions. They had never had contact with off-world beings, so of course they would be skeptical. Only a few minutes ago, she had been in disbelief that she was being asked to help. If she could still be shocked even with all the information she had, then of course they would be. Besides, she was the one having the experiences, not them. If they had been told for their entire lives that aliens were dangerous people-haters, then of course they wouldn't share her excitement. It made no sense to welcome something that was going to dominate or destroy you. Olive realized she was now in the exact same position of not believing what she was hearing. This was another lesson, wasn't it? Sometimes it seemed the universe knew exactly what it was doing.

Avratar had said time was limited, and she believed him. She wondered how long it would be before they arrived. How long would it take to write a book? She figured the book had to come before the ships came. There probably would still be a lot of fear, especially if one believed the movies, but maybe the book would be able to provide a few answers.

Olive figured the light beings would arrive with or without the book being published in time. It wasn't that they needed the book to come to help, but it would make their job easier if people weren't scared. She allowed herself a quick fantasy about having all who had doubted her line up to apologize when they saw the ships.

"People are going to want to know some details. I mean, a lot of people have seen strange lights in the sky and even seen things up close. There's tons of information online about people's experiences. It's probably helpful that the Pentagon has confessed that UFOs are real and that they've been studying them for years. And I suppose it helps that many scientists agree that life on other planets is pretty much guaranteed. So what will happen? What will people see? Will there be flying saucers or what?"

"Yes, there will be many vehicles in your skies," Avratar said. "Some will be quite large—large enough to contain many smaller flying craft. Some of the smaller craft may land on Earth for direct contact with humans. There will also be many different shapes and configurations."

"When will everything happen? Is there a specific date or what?"

"As you might imagine, a project of this magnitude requires considerable coordination. We are finalizing some aspects of the project now. It will be soon."

"So what are you and all the others going to do? I mean, are you able to clean up all the pollution? Do you have technology to fix global warming? Can you repair the ozone layer?"

"I understand that you wish to have details, but now is not the time to discuss the specifics. There will be ample time for information when we arrive."

Olive's mind was racing. She wasn't sure which questions to ask Avratar before she started to plan what to write. She realized that at some point, she had made the quantum leap from being resistant to writing a book to being excited to play even a small part in this huge event.

"What if people are terrified?" she asked.

"We will still be coming to help," he replied. "They may not initially understand, but we will be very present until our task has been completed."

"Are you just coming to the United States, to North America, to—"

"There will be ships above every populated area on Earth."

All over Earth? Olive gasped when she realized how many craft would need to be involved. "So if the multidimensional people are on a different frequency, we probably couldn't see them, could we? But the beings from other planets are the ones coming on the ships, so that's why we would see them?" Olive still wasn't sure about the difference between multidimensionals and ETs. "Is that why I've been seeing the ETs for the last year or so? So I can help communicate how they want to help?"

"That is one purpose, yes."

"But, Avratar, I still don't understand why I was picked to do this," Olive said. "I mean, of course I want to help, but why me?"

"Olive Stuart, you have experienced many frightening events in your life. There were experiences you do not recall that you had when you were very young, when you were four years old. I am aware that you have no conscious recollection of those events, yet those experiences formed the basis for the development of your fearful nature throughout your life. Holding this energy of fear in your subconscious, in your emotional field, has operated like a beacon, attracting the attention of similar negative energies. Recall our conversations that one will energetically attract the energies that one focuses on. If you start the day believing you will have a bad day, you will probably end the day by discovering you were correct. If you believe you will experience a joy-filled day, you will seek experiences that validate that belief.

"Do you recall being the target of a spiteful earthbound spirit when you resided in your parents' house? You were not aware that broadcasting anxiety on the etheric plane lowered your vibratory field to the level of those entities who vibrated at the same low frequency. You wondered why your siblings did not have the same frightening experiences. They did not share your childhood experiences and did not hold your fears; therefore, they did not attract the same low-frequency entities.

"Do you also recall when you purchased your house and had the experience of unseen visitors coming into your bedroom? It was your first time living without roommates. Your parents sincerely believed they were protecting you with their frequent warnings about the dangers of living alone, stressing the need for constant vigilance due to the ever-present threats to your security. Even though you employed adequate safety measures, you began to presume you were actually in danger. Your fears that something bad might happen to you became like a self-fulfilling prophecy, as those fears actually attracted the unwanted attention of low-vibration, mischievous beings. The more you reacted to their activities, the more fear you exhibited and the more they enjoyed continuing their contact. Do you remember why those nighttime visits stopped?"

Olive figured it was because Artie had moved in, but then she realized the visitations had stopped long before they got married. "It was when I got angry, wasn't it?" Olive asked. "The nighttime visits stopped when I yelled at them to go away because I wasn't going to be afraid anymore."

"You are correct, Olive Stuart. You are to be commended. Now look at the other fears you have also faced and overcome. You have demonstrated great courage in following your own path, not the one dictated by your parents, your church, or your friends. You have followed your heart, even when others did not understand or agree. You were told to fear all Reptilians, yet your own experiences have shown you that this fear is unfounded. You have triumphed over many limiting beliefs and have therefore succeeded in aligning with higher vibrations.

"You ask why you were picked. You will be able to effectively communicate with those who will see our arrival as frightening because at one time, you shared their apprehensions. You understand others' fears because you have unearthed and then released your own fears. Your experiences will serve as an example to others, assisting them in recognizing how to fully embrace their life potential through release of limiting thoughts.

"This is why your book will tell your story. Let them know you understand. Help them to also move beyond trepidation to a place of peace, joy, and acceptance. Please help them to understand that we are coming to help."

Chapter 24

No Reason to Fear

....

"Hey, there," said Artie, taking off his coat. "What are you doing sitting in the dark?"

"It was kind of a big day. I just felt like I needed to make sense of some things. Want to join me?"

Artie sat next to her on the couch, now holding a glass of red wine. He would have offered a glass to Olive, but she'd stopped drinking anything alcoholic a long time ago. She stared wistfully at what was probably merlot. She still missed sipping a fine wine, but nothing tasted good to her anymore. Even a little bit of beer or bourbon made her physically ill. She had given up almost all meat and had cut way back on desserts. If ascension meant giving up foods because they no longer tasted good, why couldn't it have been brussels sprouts?

"I met with Avratar today and found out why they are coming. I also learned what I am supposed to do. It was a lot to take in." Olive asked Artie if he would listen to the recording she had made.

"Wow," he said as the recorder clicked off. "Wow. It all makes sense, though, don't you think? There are so many problems on Earth that we probably couldn't fix them on our own. We've screwed up the air, water, and soil so much that we don't even remember what it was like before. People fight more than they get along. And if there's a chance we might even blow up the planet, then I can see that they can't take that risk."

"You know how I take a really long time to decide things? I knew right away that he was telling the truth. And when he said there would be huge ships surrounding the planet—"

"Yeah." Artie finished her thought. "I don't think either of us had any idea how big this really was. And you don't know when this is going to happen?"

Olive shook her head. "He said it would be soon. But he's said that before. Remember 'Soon arrive' as one of my first messages? Today I was wondering if he was using the word *soon* in galactic terms, which I figured could mean light-years. I was kind of kidding when I was thinking that, but then I heard him say slowly, 'No. Earth time.' He wasn't joking, Artie."

"I'm really proud of you that you were asked to write about all of this. What kind of book are you going to write? Have you thought about what you going to say?"

His support was one of the things Olive loved most about Artie. From the first time Olive had heard, "It's time," to all of the things she had told him about Avratar, Artie never had disbelieved a word she said. He was relentlessly supportive.

"You'll finally get to use that degree as an English teacher." He grinned, ducking as a throw pillow was tossed at him.

"He wants me to help people understand how much they want to help. They don't want people to be afraid. I guess I was asked because I've dealt with so many of my own fears. He thinks maybe people will believe me. But what if they don't?"

"Like he said, they're coming whether you accept them or not. I hope that governments don't try to do anything stupid, like try to blow them up or anything. My guess is that wouldn't be a good idea."

"But what if people think it's like that radio show *War of the Worlds*? That was fiction and only a radio program, and people still got scared," she said, and even in the dark, Artie could tell Olive was starting to get anxious. "How do I get people not to assume they're coming in to take over Earth or something? What if people see it as some kind of invasion?"

Artie drained the last drops from his glass and said, "From what I know, they've actually been on Earth for a long time, right? Like thousands or maybe millions of years? And they're only now telling people that we're going to be seeing them and giving some really good reasons for why they're coming in. Does that sound like a secret invasion? If they wanted to take over Earth, wouldn't they have done it by now?"

Olive agreed he was probably right, but she couldn't help but worry about everyone's reaction. It had taken her years to accept that there really was life on other planets and in other dimensions, and she was still dealing with many questions. What was going to happen if a huge mothership just appeared?

Artie tried another approach. "Like Avratar said, they're coming to help whether you're afraid of them or not."

Olive knew Artie was being pragmatic, and he was probably right, but she was still worried about how she could reach as many people as possible.

He leaned over to give Olive a hug and a kiss.

Yep, definitely merlot.

Chapter 25

Preparing the Heart

....

"How's it going, babe?" Artie looked over Olive's shoulder at the laptop. "It looks like you're on a roll."

"Yeah," she replied, pausing from her typing. "It really helps to just tell my story and not have to make anything up. But I'm stuck on the ending. I haven't been told any of the details of how they're going to help, just that they're coming. I'm okay with that, especially since I have no idea how they're going to do it. But I keep thinking. They're all coming here to clean things up, but what happens when they leave? Will people go back to pouring poisons into the water and the earth; killing themselves with drugs; or, worse, killing each other? Will everyone just go back to the way it was before they came in to help, or will society learn some kind of lesson, and life will be different? It feels like we should all be doing something. Shouldn't we be doing something to prepare for their arrival?

"I also wonder if life will change afterward. Will life be better for people who are hungry and homeless? What about all the people who are desperately trying to leave civil wars and famine? Will we start taking care of each other instead of grabbing as much as we can for ourselves and not worrying about anyone else?

"But here's what's really bugging me. You and I aren't the ones who are dumping chemicals into the rivers or starting wars in other countries. We aren't destroying the rain forest or spraying crops with pesticides. We don't have a choice about being constantly bombarded with 5G or microwave signals. We don't even know which foods are genetically modified or what's really in our drinking water. I don't want my life completely dependent on AI, but I may not have a choice since everything seems to be going that way. And another thing: What if it's true that we really don't have to rely on coal or oil and that there are plenty of inventions that developed clean energy, but we just aren't using them? What if it's true that the big energy companies know about the inventions but can't make money on free energy so would rather dump toxins into the environment and do business as usual? I keep thinking about all the ways the visitors could help and all the ways we would probably screw everything up again when they leave.

"It just doesn't seem fair. How are we going to fix things if the people in control don't buy into finding real solutions? What if everything just goes back to the way it was after they leave? I'm just worried that after a while, we'll be back in the same situation. Does that make sense?"

Artie pulled up a chair next to her. "I don't know. Maybe they'll also give us a to-do list."

"Well, I hope they give that to-do list to the people who can do something about it. It won't do much good to give it to me."

"I'm not sure I agree about that," Artie said thoughtfully. "I hear what you're saying, but I think the message they probably want to leave us is that everyone needs to change."

"Artie, we already buy organic. We support lots of nonprofits that help people. We recycle. You use vinegar on the weeds in our yard. I can't change the world. What else are we supposed to do?"

"Yeah, I know, but listen to me for a minute. You know how you're always saying that a project won't get done if you give it to a committee? 'If you want to bury something, you send it to a committee.' You always say that all the time, because you think that if you give a project to a big group, then nobody has to take individual responsibility for it. The bigger the group, the harder it is to get something done. Right? It's like 'If the project doesn't get done, it's not my fault, because the whole group didn't do it.' Are you following me? So what if giving a giant to-do list to a government is like sending something to a committee?"

Olive stared at him as if he were speaking a foreign language. "Huh?"

Artie persisted. "So what if every single person already has a to-do list? You always say that people need to take personal responsibility, right? You just said you couldn't change the world, but what if you could? What if every one of us believed we could?"

"I hear what you're saying, but I still don't understand. I'm supposed to take personal responsibility for destroying the ozone layer? Like it's my fault?"

"But it is your fault. And it's my fault. And everybody who uses aerosols. And everybody who owns a company that pollutes. It's all of us who are the problem, and it's all of us who are the solution. Maybe that's how we need to change our thinking. We've been thinking that others need to come up with solutions. It's like we've given the most important projects to a committee, and that's why nothing has gotten done. Pollution keeps getting worse, glaciers keep melting, and people are still being tortured and starving all over the world. What if every single one of us has a to-do list to change the way we're all thinking? Even the ones who can make a difference. Actually, especially the ones who can make a difference."

"Wouldn't that be wonderful?" Olive was starting to understand. "I wonder if they're going to do that. Maybe they can tell us what to do."

Artie shook his head. "You still aren't getting it. You can't say, 'I wonder if they're going to do that,' like you're assuming we don't have to have any personal responsibility. We all got ourselves into this mess, and each one of us can do something to help get us out of it. Even if it's a small change, at least it's something. I don't think the visitors want to have to keep coming back."

There was a slight prickly feeling at the top of Olive's head. At first, it was just a little ticklish; then it got so intense that Olive made a face as she started scratching. "I think Avratar likes where this is going."

"Look at everything that has happened to you over the past few years. You stopped being afraid of everything, and now look at how much more confident and how much happier you are. You really think about putting meaning and purpose into everything you do, and now you don't seem to be worried about things as much as you used to be. Don't you remember how anxious you were years ago? Actually—now, don't get mad at me— you're even nicer than you were when I first met you." He waited for the expected response to his last comment. "What if this is what we are supposed to be doing to help the planet? Sure, everyone is supposed to be doing that—the Golden Rule, the Ten Commandments, and all that stuff—but what if this is so important that our future literally depends on it?"

"Hmm, I think you're onto something. Avratar thinks so too," Olive said, scratching at her crown again. "Okay, I totally understand that would make the world a better place, but what if it's more than that? I keep thinking about what Avratar said about how important the soul was. If the purpose of being on Earth was for the soul to have experiences and if those experiences determined if you learned lessons or not, what if it wasn't just a good idea? What if your soul depended on how you treated others?"

"What if everything depended on it?"

"Yeah. What if everything depended on it?"

One eye struggled to open wide enough to check the clock: 3:00 a.m. Artie was doing his little squeak next to her, and her crown was tingling. "Hello, Avratar."

"Good morning, Olive Stuart. You were discussing if it might be advisable to prepare for our arrival. You are to be commended for your suggestions. Yes, it is true that the most important aspect for this coming event is the willingness of each person to review his or her own stories. We have not yet discussed this, but there will be changes associated with our appearance on your planet. Those who are best prepared emotionally and spiritually will be most appreciative of our efforts.

"Many cultures have foretold of this time period in Earth's history, calling it the Shift of the Ages. Do you know why this period has been termed so? It is because some of the planetary changes that have been foretold are only witnessed every twenty-five thousand years. Every planet and all beings within the cosmos are now entering this transformative cycle, realigning energies and awareness to attain higher levels of consciousness. You and your fellow humans will have the opportunity to be part of this event.

"Earth will be experiencing a physical evolution, a rebalancing of sorts. Gaia will find herself at a significant crossroads as she expands into higher aspects of herself. She often describes this coming cycle as a stretching as she reaches her consciousness toward enhanced awareness. You have already witnessed the beginnings of physical changes on your planet, with an increase in the scale of hurricanes, tornados, earthquakes, typhoons, and extreme weather patterns. Gaia will continue to stretch as the sun begins to also express itself through increased solar flares and microbursts of energy. This transformative process will furthermore manifest as a spiritual revolution for all humans. It will initially demonstrate as a shift in consciousness, a change from a focus on the egocentric self to an expansive and powerful connection to oneness. The recalibration for each individual will be an acceleration of one's union with Source. It will be a celebration. You are seeing signs of this recalibration in your own life, are you not? Your husband said as much this evening. The changes you are seeing in your own life are very similar to the changes also experienced by others with whom you feel a compatibility. This is not a coincidence, as those of similar awareness are experiencing this cycle in similar ways."

"So this all good?" Was she perhaps too sleepy to fully absorb what he was saying? "I mean, if there will be natural disasters, isn't that a bad thing?"

"It is true that there will be some who will be challenged by this cycle. Those who are most aligned with the vibration of compassion for others as well as oneself will be the least likely to experience the transition as challenging. Those whose focus is primarily directed at the acquisition of money and power and the control of others may have a more difficult experience. This is why it is advisable to prepare one's heart for the Shift of the Ages."

"But how do I prepare my heart? How do I help Artie so we can go through this together?" She was now wide awake, trying to figure out what she needed to do. "What happens if Artie is prepared and I'm not? What happens to people who aren't prepared? Wait a minute. This is really about the soul, isn't it? It all goes back to the soul, doesn't it?"

"Olive Stuart, you and your husband need not be concerned. Your souls continue to align with the mission of this divine project. Your transition toward this monumental period began many years ago, when I first greeted you in your friends' living room and told you, 'It's time.' Since that time, you have been guided to greater awareness of your own abilities through the new healing skills you acquired. You are deeply connected to your spiritual purpose as well as those who are working to prepare you. Your compassion for others as well as Gaia is well noted and deeply appreciated. Your role is now to help educate others."

"Won't the book do that?"

"The book will be one avenue. There will be other vehicles as well. We will address all opportunities for growth at a future time when your vessel is more receptive."

Her vessel was still deep in thought when the first rays of daylight appeared.

Ten members of Starseed sat in the circle, silently digesting all that Olive had told them. Over the years, each person had privately shared with Olive his or her experiences; many events had been confusing, frightening, or exciting. Now they were telling others. Olive knew what that felt like. Some confessed they didn't feel Earth was their home and were homesick for their families and their true selves. Some spoke of having continuing contacts with nonhumans, including some they could see and communicate with and some that were more like floating orbs of light or maybe plasma energies. Two had seen UFOs and believed there had been communication with the occupants. A couple people had had abduction experiences. Several, like Olive, remembered being from a different race in a previous lifetime. Each person came to the group with his or her own belief system but also a shared knowing that they were part of something larger than themselves.

There was an undercurrent of excitement and anticipation, as they all felt they were on the verge of finding answers to all the questions they had been asking: "Who am I? What am I doing here? What is my life purpose? What am I supposed to be doing to help others?" Olive felt as if everything in her own life had led up to this moment.

"So that's why I thought we needed to come together to help figure all of this out. I need your help," she said. "I was told that my part in all this was to write the book that will hopefully help take away fears and maybe give people some of the answers they're looking for. I'm on the last chapter now. That's why I've been hidden away for a few months.

"But there's more. We've been asked to do more than just write a book. We've been asked to be lighthouses. Sometimes they're called nodes. I think this means we are supposed to be anchors, like central information centers, to get the word out to people and then, when things really start to happen, to help them adjust to whatever recalibration looks like. Maybe this is like what is called holding space. I don't know. It sounds like it may not be easy for everyone."

"What if they don't want to hear?" Stan asked.

"I asked that too," Olive responded. "And Avratar said that our primary responsibility is to those who understand and who are asking for support. We can't be accountable for everyone, especially those who have no idea what the book is talking about. We're only supposed to be helping those who want our help."

"What happens to the ones who don't understand, don't want to know, or think we're crazy?" Mildred asked.

"I don't know," Olive answered truthfully. "I still haven't really gotten an answer on that. I'm pretty sure there will be those who just don't get it. Hey, we all have people in our own families who don't get it, right? Sometimes I think they don't believe in anything other than money, power, and what is right in front of them. I do kind of wonder how an atheist might react to all of this."

Shaking her head, she added, "I know I've been up to my eyeballs in all this, but I've even still wondered if maybe none of this is real. What if I'm really not seeing things or knowing things or talking to light beings? What if this is all in my imagination? But then I realize that many of you have gotten the same information from another being, haven't you? And my friend in Virginia told me she got almost identical information, even though we've never talked about this before. In fact, she'd never talked to anybody before she asked me what I'd been up to and I got the courage to tell her. Man, I wish you could have seen her face. But yeah, I still have times when I wonder if somebody's messing with us. But I keep going back to a discussion I had with Avratar about faith. And this is just me talking, I do believe. I probably won't have proof until the first motherships show up. I guess he's right that everybody has to follow his or her own path."

"If we're supposed to be information centers or nodes, how will people find us?" Shirley asked. She lived about ninety minutes away and was already wondering how she could be a node in her area. "Walter lives about an hour away from here in the other direction."

"Sometimes I suspect this is why all of us were directed to the Center," Olive said. "We were told more than once that the people who needed to be here would be sent here. Look at the number of people who show up saying, 'I don't know why I'm here. I just had the feeling I had to talk to someone.' Maybe this is the beginning of creating a network of nodes. Maybe the Center is at the middle, kind of like a hub, and everyone fans out from here. What if this was the plan all along—to bring us all together?"

Marianne was thoughtful. She had been the channel during many of Avratar's appearances and suggested the group needed to focus on his primary message. "If all of us have been given a mandate to prepare our hearts and if we need to help others to do that, I think we need to give them specific suggestions. There are going to be people who have no idea what 'Prepare your heart' even means."

"We have no idea how much time we have to get ready for their arrival," Olive said. "So what is the most important information people will need to know? How can we all best prepare for what Avratar and the others have said will happen?"

There would be questions, which could be answered on the website. What if people wanted to talk to someone in person?

"Just about all of us have seen ourselves on a stage in front of a lot of people, right? Maybe through dreams or visions or someone telling us in an intuitive message," Olive said. "I think we'll be asked to go to conferences. Maybe we'll be interviewed. We don't know how many other people have gotten the information we have. Maybe a lot of people but maybe no one."

There was general agreement that the biggest concern was how to help people prepare their hearts. Everyone interpreted that to mean being more heart-centered in connecting to each other, the environment, and him- or herself. There was a focus on spirituality and the search for finding meaning and purpose in one's own life. No, no one in the circle questioned what that phrase meant, especially since every class and every service at the Center had that as its goal. Actually, finding purpose was what originally had drawn everyone to the Center. It wasn't enough to just exist; they all wanted to put meaning into their lives.

But now the challenge would be to connect with and offer support to those who had no idea what spiritual development work even was. There were people who were so busy making a living that they never thought about making a life. There were those who didn't see a reason to think about meaning and purpose, or perhaps they believed the meaning and purpose of their lives was to make money or control others. Maybe they never spent a moment even wondering if they had a soul.

Just as being spiritual was a foreign concept for many people, the idea of not being spiritual was equally foreign to the Starseed members. This would be a challenge.

Questions arose that made the challenge even more problematic: What if people didn't want to hear how any of this mattered in their everyday lives? What if they didn't want to know? How could Starseed help them if they turned their backs on them?

Someone said, "Wait a minute. We've already been told that there will be people we can't reach. It's not our role to convince people to suddenly think about meaning and purpose, especially if they think we're crazy. I think our role is to help the people who ask us to help them. We'll probably be plenty busy with that group."

"I agree," Olive said, and she asked the group what it meant to them to be heart-centered and how they would suggest explaining the concept to those who wanted to know.

There was general agreement that most people made decisions primarily with logic and analytical thinking. As Olive noted, "Actually, one website said that ninety to ninety-five percent of people are considered left-brain thinkers, which means they tend to be more methodical, objective, and pragmatic in their approach to problem-solving. Their approach focuses on 'Does it make sense? Does it physically serve me? If I marry that person, I will have a secure financial future and a beautiful house. If I take that job, I will make a lot of money.'

"But the focus for heart-centered people is instead on the feelings associated with an issue. For example, 'Would taking the job or marrying that person make me happy and fulfilled?' Listening to your heart incorporates emotion, creativity, and meaning and a critical balance to making decisions only through logic. Making important decisions without giving your heart a vote may result in adequate money, safe housing, and a secure future, but it doesn't take into consideration whether you would find joy in that marriage, house, or job.

"The heart-centered people would be more likely to understand the concept of oneness, extending the awareness to animals, the planet, and nonhuman beings. They probably think about their own soul and may even have considered the possibility of their soul having past or future lives. Many heart-centered people believe in angels and other divine messengers; receive intuitive messages, often in meditation; and believe there is a purpose or mission for their lives.

"On the other hand, the left-brained, analytical, methodical people would possibly reject the concept of life on other planets as well as the probability of ever being personally contacted by an off-world being. They often reject the concept of unseen messengers or helpers or any divine influence or support. They probably have never had a Reiki session, an intuitive guidance session, or anything that connects to Source."

"I think we're supposed to work with the middle group," Shirley said. "The ones who maybe have already had experiences or accept the idea of ETs don't really need us. The ones who are positive there's no such thing as life on other planets or have no interest in becoming heart-centered won't take our help anyway. I think we're supposed to work with the ones who are open, want to change, and want our help."

As there was general agreement, suggestions were offered to prepare the heart for the coming shift in consciousness, beginning with channeled messages from Avratar and Chardon, another light being who was in regular contact with Marianne.

Avratar began. "To prepare the heart is no small thing. This is very much the essence of who you are and how you are. As you ascend and as you move in densities and consciousness, preparing your heart is like preparing a garden or an area for growth of plants. So as you prepare the soil, you think first about removing things that get in the way—rocks, old roots, and materials that don't need to be there. Consider, if you will, that preparing your heart is removal of some things. For example, you need to remove the fears that live there, the fears that get in the way of your being able to believe and being able to move your belief system. You need to be able to remove unforgiveness and to remove judgments. These things build barriers or walls between you and others.

"If you are to become interconnected and see that interconnection, you have to be able to remove those barriers that keep you from seeing another as another versus what is currently done, which is to see another as separate, somehow less than or more than but separate and different. But you are all part of the same energy, part of the same tapestry.

"The other part that will assist you in this process is to remove your desire to consistently categorize and affix a title or label to something or someone. Those are very mind-centric approaches. Heart-centric approaches are to dissolve the barriers between you and others. To dissolve the need to fix, solve, or resolve. Or to assist or to help. Those are thought by some to be noble causes—to help, to support. But when they come from a space of a hierarchy or a sense of obligation or responsibility, they impede your progress. They impede your ability to connect. When you dissolve the barriers between yourself and others, when you dissolve your separation and isolation, you begin to see that the person, that being, is just another part of the manifestation of you. So dissolving those boxes you have, dissolving the separation you have, and dissolving even the sense of your own self and identity is not to lose yourself but to understand your integration—how you are woven into everything and how everything and everyone is woven into you."

Someone asked Avratar what would be the best way to begin. He replied, "You must stop the pursuit of busyness, the pursuit that takes your time and your focus and pulls your heart into a dark space. Preparing your heart requires disconnecting. It requires quiet; it requires some inward focus. There are many ways you have to do this. You see them in the world as meditation, prayer, contemplation, reflection, journaling and other writing, artwork and carpentry, running, biking, and other forms of exercise that allow one to focus and to move away from the busyness of the world. Being out in the trees, mountains, oceans, deserts, and forests—the places where you may be washed by the energy of the natural beings that are there—is one of the most profound and straightforward ways."

Chardon added, "Preparing your heart is also something that may be done in a collective, a group. You may amplify the power and the connection by joining with another or more than one—multiples perhaps. Things such as your group meditations you have done. Or hike together, as you have done. A group that is creating music together, for example, and intentionally connecting and dissolving the bonds between them to come together would be another way."

Starseed members thanked Avratar and Chardon and then added their own suggestions.

Stan said, "Release fear. Experiencing fear is a normal human response, but if you choose not to deal with those fears, they will ultimately control your life by changing your behavior, your relationships, and every part of your world. The hardest part about fear is identifying how and why it has impacted you, as sometimes the original event that provoked the fear has either been long forgotten or discounted as unimportant.

"We all hold fears of some kind, whether or not you label it as such. Sometimes the fear can be traced to a specific event or person. Maybe someone hurt you, or you have a painful memory of having run out of gas in an unsafe neighborhood. Sometimes memories from childhood can still impact your behavior as an adult. For example, someone broke into our house when I was a child, so now I have ten locks on my doors and windows and check each one compulsively.

"Think about all the things you don't enjoy or perhaps absolutely refuse to do. Is there a fear attached to this? If you are afraid of enclosed spaces, you might walk up twenty flights of stairs rather than getting into an elevator. If you are afraid of heights, you might never plan a vacation to a faraway place, for fear of being on an airplane. Being unable to swim safely as a child may mean you avoid being near large bodies of water as an adult or perhaps hate taking baths.

"Perhaps, like Olive, many of your fears were passed down to you from parents or society. Have you ever thought about why you are uncomfortable with people of a certain religion or ethnic group? Did an older sibling once scare you, and now you hate darkness, snakes, or insects? Did someone make fun of something you said when you were young, and now you hate public speaking or even standing up for yourself?

"The most effective way to release your fears is first of all to acknowledge them. Are you afraid to be alone or perhaps of being lonely? There's a difference. Have you been called a hypochondriac, when perhaps you have memories of loved ones who died without wanting to see a doctor? Are you afraid of dogs because you were once bitten? Do thunderstorms produce a panic attack?

"Once you recognize what you most want to avoid, you can look at the issue more objectively. What happens when you have the experience?

Do you avoid the situation—for example, never going into that store again? Or is your response full-blown anxiety or even terror? Do you have a recurring nightmare?"

Olive remembered that when she was very young, she had a girlfriend who once vomited after she happened to eat something peppermint. "Now the adult woman feels nauseated every time she smells peppermint. When you're ready to move beyond the fear, you can consider natural therapies, such as emotional freedom techniques, including tapping, which give you tools to reclaim your power. You might even consider that the fear is not based in this lifetime. Science has validated that phobias can travel through DNA for multiple generations; a past-life regression can be helpful in releasing fears that may have originated with your grandparents. What if your great-great-grandfather was actually the one who was terrified of being attacked by bears?

"Remember, if you do not control your fears, your fears will control you. Welcome the wisdom of the soul and the spirit."

Stan said, "For me, 'Prepare your heart' is connecting with and opening your heart center to the wisdom of the soul and spirit. To transcend the lower, darker emotional frequencies and embrace love and gratitude in thought, word, and deed through conscious intention. It is by connecting with the heart and expressing the heart energy that our own vibrations shift upward and allow us to ascend to higher-consciousness living. The heart is the doorway, the bridge, to connecting with our higher selves and the higher selves of others on this 3D plane and beyond.

"By preparing the heart, we allow ourselves to move through and beyond the baggage we have carried from past pain, trauma, and disappointment and to embrace the goodness within ourselves and others. It is about healing these experiences and finding your way back to your authentic self, peeling the layers back to get to the core of who you are. I think of this as a road to wholeness, where you choose to walk down this path of self-exploration and healing, stopping when you need to or taking time to see the sights on your journey. Some may get lost or distracted but can intentionally choose to search for the path back to wholeness.

"From this shift, we become aware of higher light energies flowing through us. We discover soul gifts that open us to greater capacities of love, empathy, and insight to ourselves and others. We gain tools to become more aware of and manage the different energies and entities we encounter as we grow and ascend in our own being. Further, we are more capable and prepared to protect against lower-frequency energies and entities that are attracted to our higher-frequency light."

They went on to suggest practices that could help open the heart and expand heart-centered consciousness.

"Perform meditation and self-reflection on situations and experiences that you associate with lower-frequency emotions, such as disappointment, anger, guilt, jealousy, hate, rage, and envy, and seek to understand why these emotions are generated."

"Work with energetic healing modalities, such as Reiki, to identify and shift energy blocks in the energy systems."

"Learn to sense your energy field and the fields of others."

"Learn about the chakras and their energetic role for your physical, emotional, mental, and spiritual bodies."

"Practice self-care and make adjustments to lifestyle that are healthier and more beneficial for your spiritual growth."

"Intentionally connect with your concept of Source or God on a regular basis."

"Learn about and experience the different spiritual guides and helpers available to you for growth and support."

"Participate in practices that help to ground, center, and clear your energy and maximize your presence and growth."

"Create sacred space where your vibration is raised and supported."

"Connect with elemental energies for balance and spiritual support."

"Give back in gratitude. Share your gifts with those who accept them, whether through volunteer work or by actively seeking to deepen family and friend relationships."

"Express forgiveness and gratitude in your relationships with others as well as yourself."

"Learn how intention can program our experience and how to live intentionally instead of by reaction."

"Learn to uncover and heal from the subconscious programming, beliefs, psychological patterns, and traumas that limit our access and expression of our authentic selves."

"Connect with the emotion of success. There are countless books and practices that encourage you to create a positive affirmation, first identifying what you most want in life and then visualizing that you already have it. Many people use the phrases 'I'm happy' or 'I am surrounded by abundance' to begin the process. While that technique is certainly part of the process, the most important element in the creation of an effective affirmation is how much you emotionally connect to the outcome. Do you really want to be happy, or do you secretly believe you aren't worthy? Do you really want to attain wellness, or would you miss the attention and sympathy if you were no longer sick? Affirmations can be quickly self-sabotaged if you can't imagine ever attaining what you want or believe you don't deserve it."

"Choose to be happy. Have you ever wondered why some people seem to have a sunny, outgoing disposition, and others live under a dark cloud? The positive people know the secret to happiness: their life is determined not by what has happened to them but by how they have chosen to respond to what happened to them. Everyone has had experiences that have angered or hurt him or her. But this is actually a self-fulfilling prophecy; you get to choose whether you want to continue to harbor ill feelings or get over it and move on. If you make the conscious decision to choose peace, the extra benefit is that you will automatically also invite happiness. Remember, Abraham Lincoln once said, 'Most people are about as happy as they make up their minds to be.'"

"Feel gratitude. Have you ever met someone who seemed to have an amazing life, but all she or he did was complain? Perhaps she or he is attractive, with a good job and what appears to be a happy family, but your friend can only find the dark side to a situation. When you feel gratitude, you get to recall specific reasons for being thankful. Maybe you didn't get the promotion, but you still have a job you enjoy. Maybe someone forgot your birthday, but you know that person loves you every day. Maybe the furnace takes a while to warm up your house in the morning, but you have a house, and it has a furnace; many people don't have that luxury. The more you focus on what you have instead of what you do not, the more joy you radiate."

"Show compassion. So much of the world now is polarized into an us-versus-them mentality, believing that others are somehow very different from us. The reality is that everyone experiences dark moments and hopelessness at some point, but we rarely are aware of it. Aches, pains, and serious illnesses often are not obvious, but we can be critical of those who appear able-bodied yet park in handicapped parking spaces. We know how debilitating stress and anxiety can feel, filling us with foreboding, fear, and worry, but we sometimes don't sympathize with others who might also be overwhelmed. Compassion is the foundation of most of the world's major religions: 'Treat others as you would like to be treated.'"

"Forgive. Holding resentment and wishing vengeance are the fastest ways to shut down your heart center, keeping you in a constant cycle of victimization and pain. However, extending forgiveness can be the fastest way to reclaim your power. Forgiveness does not mean you forget the wrong done to you; it means you will not permit the wrong or the one who perpetrated it to define you any longer. Letting that person know you will no longer allow yourself to connect to the pain you received will generate a wholeness to your soul. And when you search your soul for ways to forgive, please first and foremost forgive yourself for anything you have done—or did not do—that you may still regret. Remember, forgiveness is the healing that you give to yourself."

"Follow your passion. How many of us have looked with envy at someone who reached a life goal? We admire his or her hard work and long hours, but rarely do we have an awareness of what has truly propelled each person to success: passion. Each of us has dreams and desires, but fears often prevent us from transforming those hopes into fulfillment. The emotion of envisioning your successful future creates the energy through which the universe works to fulfill those dreams. How sad to regret not following your passion when you perform your end-of-life review."

Chapter 26

Arrival

....

"Good afternoon," Artie said as Olive finally emerged from slumber.

"No fooling. It took forever to fall asleep last night," Olive replied, reaching for her favorite coffee mug. "I was wide awake for hours."

"It wasn't a full moon, was it? I know that's rough on you."

"No, it was more like I was a little kid on the night before Christmas. I just felt like my body wouldn't relax. Good thing I was planning on going in a little later today."

"Well, I'm not," Artie replied, giving her a kiss, and he headed for the door. "See you when I see you."

She was almost resentful of the time wasted while she lay awake in bed. It didn't happen often, but when it did, she was usually too tired to meditate or do Reiki on herself but not awake enough to get up and do anything productive. She took another sip and felt the gentle caffeine buzz that was just starting to keep her eyes open.

She wondered if anything at last night's Starseed meeting had kept her awake. They had been meeting regularly for about seven months, usually comparing messages they had been receiving, both individually and in the group meditations, as well as planning their next steps. At first, only a few of them had heard that the light beings would be arriving soon; now almost all the members were getting contacted with similar information. Some of their messages were in dreams, some came through automatic writing, and some involved direct contact.

Interestingly, posts on social media indicated this was also happening all over the world. Whether it was from Europe, Japan, or the United States, the information was the same: they would arrive soon, they were coming to help, and humans should prepare their hearts. A number of UFO-tracking websites seemed to show more videos of recent sightings than they used to, but maybe she was just more tuned in to looking for them. Even so, there seemed to be a different kind of buzz lately, like anticipation or excitement. She wondered if that was what had kept her awake last night.

She liked to sit quietly in the sunroom for a few minutes each morning, sometimes just to look at the birds at the backyard feeders and sometimes to go into a deep meditation. Occasionally, Avratar or another being would connect. That morning, she kept noticing her heart was beating much faster and harder than it usually did. That usually was one of the signals that one of her unseen friends was nearby. But she didn't have a sense that anyone was trying to connect that morning, so she dismissed any possible significance. She had stopped giving too much attention to things that seemed odd in her life. Lately, it seemed everything was odd in her life.

She got ready for work and filled up her coffee cup before heading out toward her car. Her heart was pounding even more furiously. *What the heck was going on?* she thought. If she hadn't recently had a physical, she might have been concerned. *Probably something energetic*, she thought. *Like some kind of intuitive signal coming in. Strange that it suddenly got so dark out.*

She glanced up at the sky and gasped. She didn't even realize that her favorite coffee cup shattered on the sidewalk. Whatever blocked out the sun was right overhead, and it was huge.

The object stretched across her neighborhood and way beyond. But she also had the feeling it was really high in the sky, almost as if it were hovering above the clouds. *That would make it even larger*, she realized. *Maybe even miles wide.* It looked like metal, and she could see that there were things protruding from the sides. It wasn't anything like the photos she had seen of flying saucers. It almost looked like a floating city.

She stood transfixed, just staring. She had always joked she would know it was all real when the mothership appeared overhead. Her brain tried to make sense of everything she was seeing. It was real. *So what happens next?*

It was motionless. Some of the lights were slowly flashing, and a few were constantly on. Olive strained to hear the sounds of an airplane, a helicopter, or anything that might explain what she was seeing, but the neighborhood was completely silent. A cluster of neighbors stood in a front yard. Some kids with cell phones were taking photos. Two cars narrowly avoided a collision in front of her house, as the drivers were obviously watching it too. Somewhere in the distance, she heard a siren start up— like the ones used for tornado warnings. If she ever had wondered if others were able to see what she could see, she now had her answer. If this was what she thought it was, there were probably ships visible all over the world.

Now she knew why her heart was pounding so furiously and why she had been unable to get to sleep last night. A giant lump formed in her throat, and tears rolled down her cheeks.

This was the day they had been preparing for. They had arrived.

Printed in the United States
by Baker & Taylor Publisher Services